make SPACE!

design for theatre and alternative spaces

IMAGINATION
ENTERTAINMENTS

Imagination Entertainments is delighted to be able to support Make Space!. *As a designer and theatrical producer I know all too well the time and energy it takes to make a performance space come alive in new and exciting ways for the audience. Theatre Design Umbrella is to be congratulated for having the vision to create this impressive exhibition. Such a celebration of the richness and diversity of contemporary British stage and theatre design is long overdue: testimony to our guiding principle – 'Nothing is impossible!'*

Gary Withers
Creative Director

THEATRE DESIGN UMBRELLA

Theatre Design Umbrella is an association of theatre designers, technicians and architects. It draws on the resources and membership of the following organisations:

The Society of British Theatre Designers
The Association of British Theatre Technicians
The Association of Lighting Designers
British Actors Equity Association Register of Designers

We are deeply grateful to all our sponsors, from the private individuals to large organisations that have made this exhibition, its illustrated catalogue and programme of educational events possible. Our sincere thanks must be given to:

The Esmée Fairbairn Charitable Trust
The Idlewild Trust
Imagination Entertainments
John Lewis Partnership
Cameron Mackintosh Ltd
Lady Ramsbotham
The Society of British Theatre Designers
The Tussauds Group

Action Lighting
Artattack
Alan Ayckbourn
City of Drama
C T Reprographics
Delstar Engineering Ltd
Farebrother & Co (Display) Ltd
Nicholas Hytner Charitable Trust
G H Lucking & Son
IKEA
J & C Joel Ltd
M & M
Mainstage Lighting
P L Parsons & Co Ltd
Stephen Pyle Workshops
Roscolab Ltd
Leopold de Rothschild Charitable Trust
Rotring
Royal Exchange Theatre
Samuelson Communications Ltd
Stage Electrics (North) Ltd
Talbot Designs Ltd
Technical Arts Course, City College, Manchester
White Light North Ltd
8 by 4 Productions Ltd

and to the following for their inspiration, commitment and practical help:

Carla Eve Amie
Ann Bates
Jan Bee Brown, Stephen Joseph Theatre in the Round
Alison Benbow
Becky Chapman, Education officer
Dean Clough Galleries
David Cockayne
Ken Coker, Technical director
Mike Dilger of The White Lion
Danny Flowers
Billy Klinger
James Langley, Royal Shakespeare Company
Ethel Langstreth
Anabel Lord, MLR
Gregory MacNeil
Manchester City Council
Dud Newall
Andrea Nixon
David Palser
Royal Northern College of Music
Sheila Schwartz
Kate Seekts
Jack Thompson

Published in Great Britain in 1994 by Theatre Design Umbrella in association with The Society of British Theatre Designers, 47 Bermondsey Street, London SE1 3XT

Text copyright © 1994

A catalogue record for this book is available from the British Library.

Designed by Lesley Smith

Printed by Shanleys, Bolton

Compiled by Kate Burnett and Peter Ruthven Hall

Edited by Phyllida Shaw and Keith Allen

CONTENTS

INTRODUCTION

This collection of theatre and stage design has been published to accompany *Make Space!* – a national exhibition taking place in Manchester, in November 1994 as one of the final events of the City of Drama celebrations.

The exhibition shows work carried out between 1990 and 1994 by designers born in Britain or who have been based in the UK for a substantial period of time. This catalogue illustrates examples of work contributed by many of those designers including set, costume and lighting designs and the design of performance spaces. Neither the exhibition nor the catalogue should be seen as a comprehensive survey of the period, but rather as a celebration of the diversity and richness of current theatre practice in the UK.

A prime task of the stage designer is to create a space in which a theatrical performance can take place; a time-frame, an environment and a context that guide and inform the audience in its appreciation and enjoyment of that performance. The visual language of design is also a fundamental part of the performance within that space.

The designer's job is to mould and sculpt the performance space in response to a variety of factors and, essentially, to negotiate the relationship between what takes place 'on stage' and the audience. In purpose-built theatres, this relationship is to some extent predetermined. In adaptable spaces and in spaces specifically chosen by the designer or director, the designer has more opportunities to create that relationship.

The use of converted buildings for performance, from former churches and cinemas to wash houses and warehouses, has become increasingly popular in the last 25 years, presenting the designer with a whole range of opportunities. Another phenomenon is the production of non-theatre performances using locations which become theatre settings in their own right – a tunnel, a shipyard or a park. Here the event engages the audience in a fusion of performance and environment.

It seems both useful and provocative to look back at five years of theatre design and architecture within the broad context of this relationship between the audience and the performance.

A stage design does not fully exist except at the moment of performance. Similarly, the architecture of a performance space is not fully expressed until it is inhabited by an audience and performers. However, both possess potential and both can demonstrate proportion, balance, resonances and significance.

The photographs and drawings of stage and theatre design in the pages that follow hint at these moments and intentions. Some of them are more striking, more photogenic than others, giving an impression perhaps that the better the image, the better the design. This is not necessarily the case. Some of the designs illustrated may be equally effective *in situ* but less tangible as a printed image. To place their images in context we invited the designers to write a few lines to accompany their images, focusing, in particular, on their response to the characteristics of the performance space.

In the process of putting together this project we have reconsidered the forms in which visual information is presented in British theatre. The contents of the exhibition and catalogue are organised in seven sections: theatres-in-the-round, purpose built adaptable spaces, thrust and open stages, proscenium theatres, touring theatre, converted spaces and event and non-theatre performances. We hope that this grouping provides a coherent and illuminating passage through an extraordinarily diverse and exciting collection of work.

THEATRES-IN-THE-ROUND

A fundamental element of theatre is the relationship between the performer and the audience. The theatres featured in this section have formalised the apparently informal shapes of spontaneous gatherings in streets, dance halls and classrooms (two of them were built from the vision of one man, Stephen Joseph). In these buildings the major elements of scenery are with us – the wrapround audience and, in the centre, the actors who create shifting points of focus within the frame we, the audience, create.

ROYAL EXCHANGE THEATRE

Manchester, 1976

The Manchester Royal Exchange ceased to function as the centre of the world's cotton market in 1968. At the same time, the '69' Theatre Company was looking for a place to build a 700-800-seat theatre.

Caspar Wrede, the Artistic Director, explained at the time: 'We need a stage that can conjure places and make time relative to the demands of drama. Other ages have had their illusions, only we have none and are contented. We need a new stage on which to wake our dreams and awake ourselves within the dream, but if we want that stage, we'll have to build it ourselves.'

It may not be overtly apparent, but all the rhythms in the theatre's structure are based on a rose. The theatre is made of tubular steel and toughened glass, based on a seven-sided figure with raked seating for 400 at ground level. The two galleries above, each seating 150, are suspended by rods from the roof trusses, which bear on four tubular shell frames anchored to the pillars supporting the main hall.

Architects: Levitt Bernstein Associates in collaboration with Richard Negri
Theatre Consultants: Theatre Projects Consultants
Structural Engineers: Ove Arup

THESE IMAGES HAVE BEEN SPONSORED BY THE ROYAL EXCHANGE THEATRE

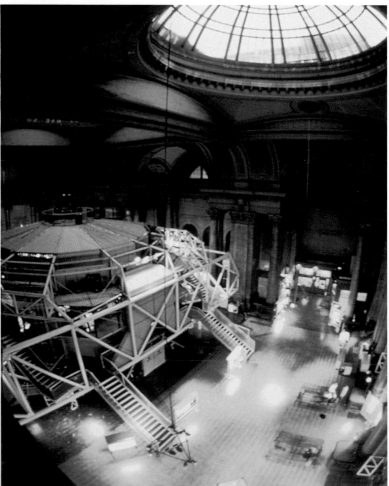

THE TEMPEST

William Shakespeare

**Royal Exchange Theatre, Manchester
September 1990**

Johanna Bryant: 'This production was conceived around Prospero's "storm in the mind". The island in the play represents his mind and the conflict between the worldly and the unworldly; between the masculine and the feminine.

'The floor of the Royal Exchange Theatre became a large pool of mirror and with the use of other reflective surfaces we were able to conjure images and "happenings" of magic, of sea changes and of appearing and disappearing protagonists. A large pink conch shell served as a feminine image for Prospero's cell and a dark, glittering, upwardly thrusting, stratified volcanic rock was Caliban's lair.

'Gentlemen's evening dress served as the springboard for costume; also being what Prospero is seen wearing in his study as the storm breaks at the beginning of the play.'

Director: Braham Murray
Designer: Johanna Bryant
Lighting designer: Robert Bryan
Choreographer and movement director: Jacky Lansley
Photo credit: Stephen Vaughan

TRINCULO.
DOUG FISHER

9

THE COMEDY OF ERRORS

William Shakespeare

Royal Exchange Theatre, Manchester
March 1993

David Short: '*Comedy of Errors* was to play alongside
Jules Feiffer's *Little Murders*, so a common basic set
was required. As there was a lot of physical action,
the main floor ended up as a large circular area of
tough, concrete-coloured carpet. This was
surrounded by a shiny area of vinyl which travelled
under the front rows of seats. The two areas were
paint-splattered to make the grey area of carpet look
as if it was growing out of the shiny black surround.
The first tier of balcony fronts was covered with
sheets of transparent corrugated plastic, also
splattered with paint. The whole effect evoked a
cold, concrete, city circus ring.

'Because the play moves at a great pace, everything
ended up on wheels. The famous scene where there
is action both inside and outside a house was solved
with a door on wheels which could be moved round
by two crew members. Large mesh screens, also on
wheels, became a customs barrier, a row of telephone
kiosks and the side of a tube train for when
Antipholus arrives in Ephesus.'

Director: Gregory Hersov
Designer: David Short
Lighting designer: Ace McCarron
Fight director: Nicholas Hall
Movement: Nigel Nicholson
Photo credit: Stephen Vaughan

Jo

Mo

BLUES FOR MR CHARLIE

James Baldwin

**Royal Exchange Theatre, Manchester
October 1992**

David Short: 'At the Royal Exchange an audience of 700 can focus around an actor on stage and see everything he does at close proximity. For the designer, most walls and doors cannot exist here, so one is guided towards creating the atmosphere an actor breathes and, in a play with numerous scenes, providing what is essential to tell the story.

'The play is based on the facts surrounding the death of Emmet Till in Mississippi in 1964. It starts with a shot in the dark and a white man dragging a dead black man across the stage. Then, in a series of flashbacks, it builds up the story of why this happened, ending in a trial.

'I felt the play needed as much air and space as possible so the floor, which looked like large worn and sandy sheets of southern yellow pine, spread flat across the stage and then gently ramped up a permanently widened exit into the darkness of the hall outside.

'Acc McCarron's minimal lighting emphasised the spaciousness. The central hanging basket which is usually packed with lanterns had only one, to light witnesses in the trial scene in Act III.'

Director: Gregory Hersov
Designer: David Short
Lighting designer: Ace McCarron
Fight director: Nicholas Hall
Musical director: Luke Smith
Photo credit: Stephen Vaughan

THE BROTHERS KARAMAZOV

Feodor Mikhailovich Dostoevsky

Royal Exchange Theatre, Manchester
February 1993

Director: Braham Murray
Designer: Simon Higlett
Lighting designer: Vince Herbert
Choreographer: Wendy Allnut
Fight director: Malcolm Ranson
Photo credit: Stephen Vaughan

THE COUNT OF MONTE CRISTO

Alexandre Dumas adapted by James Maxwell and
Jonathan Hackett

Royal Exchange Theatre, Manchester
May 1994

Vince Herbert: 'The use of brass, copper and silver mirrors as portable follow spots, operated by both crew and actors, provided almost unlimited lighting angles and added a unique colour quality to the show. Growing from this idea, a fireworks display was created by flashing large mirrors in front of chasing Parcans.

'The set consisted of a sandy mound, out of which actors and scenery appeared, and a rich, central hanging structure. The cave-like theme of the design was repeatedly emphasised by returning to the motif of cracks of broken white light.'

Director: Braham Murray
Designer: Simon Higlett
Lighting designer: Vince Herbert
Choreographers: Fergus Early and Emil Wolk
Photo credit: Stephen Vaughan

END OF THE FOOD CHAIN
Tim Firth

**Stephen Joseph Theatre in the Round
December 1993**

Jan Bee Brown: 'Kale Moor is a grocery distribution depot – the place where supermarkets go to shop. Dexion is everywhere, caging everything, stretching up into the heavens. And in every direction we are distracted by the mouth-watering attraction of excess, intensely concentrated pockets of different, recognisable, yummy foods. Food, food, everywhere, but not a drop to eat.'

Jackie Staines: 'One of the knacks to lighting in the round is to try to vary the direction of the key light as much as possible so that all members of the audience benefit equally from the work of the lighting designer. In shows requiring only a single static lighting state this is not so easy.

'In *The End of the Food Chain* the prime consideration was the choice of colour to represent low-pressure, sodium sources creating the feeling of artificial light within a general wash. For the *arty* bits of the show – the scenes on the roof and the catwalks – I used low-level lighting positions, specifically luminaires built into the set.'

Director: Connal Orton
Designer: Jan Bee Brown
Lighting designer: Jackie Staines
Design assistant: Kate Marriott
Photo credit: Adrian Gatie

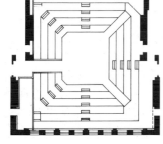

New Theatre in the Round

Scarborough

Due to open 1995

Production manager **Stefan Gleisher**: 'The Odeon Cinema is a redundant, 1700-seat, Art Deco cinema built in 1935, and a Grade II listed building. The architects, Henry Osborne Christmas Associates, originated proposals to transform the building into a new permanent home for the internationally renowned Stephen Joseph Theatre, for the playwright Alan Ayckbourn.

'Shepherd Design and Build are now creating a 400-seat theatre-in-the-round with all its associated facilities and a 165-seat studio theatre/cinema within the existing circle area, together with a restaurant, bar, box office and foyer facilities.'

Macbeth

William Shakespeare

Waterside Theatre, Stratford-Upon-Avon

The World of Shakespeare, April 1994

Vince Herbert: 'This 30-minute adaptation was totally reliant on sound and lighting to replace the missing two hours and 20 characters! Limited to 48 ways and an Arri Mirage, the lighting had to create the witches' apparitions, the battle sequences and the interiors and exteriors. I used smoke, gently fanned across the stage, to project on to and to light through. Some dialogue is delivered directly to the lighting and the lighting responds.'

Director: Robert Clare
Set designer: Samantha Jane Carver
Lighting designer: Vince Herbert
Photo credit: Bryan Torfeh

TWELFTH NIGHT

William Shakespeare

New Victoria Theatre, North Staffordshire
February 1991

Lis Evans: 'Shakespeare's subtitle *What You Will* influenced the decision to set our production amidst the culture of the psychedelic 1960s, with its sense of abandoning the normal order of things for a time. My design solution was based on a classic country house, inhabited by a kind of "rock music aristocracy". The split-levels followed the shape of the auditorium, combining Yin and Yang curves, lawn and wave patterns, with influences of 60s' culture, like *The Magic Roundabout*.'

Director: Bob Eaton
Designer: Lis Evans
Lighting designer: Paul Jones
Musical director: Greg Palmer

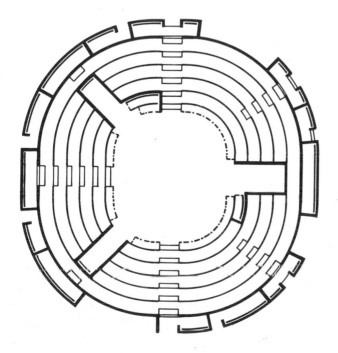

THE JOLLY POTTERS

Rony Robinson and Peter Cheeseman

New Victoria Theatre, North Staffordshire
February 1991

Lis Evans: '*The Jolly Potters* was a documentary production about the events leading up to and surrounding the Chartist riots in the Potteries in 1842. The setting was a flat-painted floorcloth with a few elements of versatile furniture used to create many different places. The simple setting allowed easy movement between the 21 scenes and access to the three entrances and two notch areas on either side of the stage. Key quotations from historical documents on which the play was based were written on large banners on the theatre walls.'

Director: Peter Cheeseman
Designer: Lis Evans
Lighting designer: Paul Jones
Composer and choreographer: John Kirkpatrick

DANGEROUS CORNER

J B Priestley

New Victoria Theatre, North Staffordshire
May 1993

Cathy Ryan: 'The New Vic is a large and tall space and sometimes that makes it difficult to present an intimate drama. We decided to shrink the stage and build it up in overlapping levels. I felt these rostra needed a strong colour and shape in order to distinguish them from the floor. The shaped levels, in curves and right angles, reflected both the themes of the play and the shape of the auditorium and, I hope, also suggested spatial relationships between the characters involved.'

Director: Peter Cheeseman
Designer: Cathy Ryan
Lighting designer: Paul Jones

NICE GIRLS

Devised by the company

New Victoria Theatre, North Staffordshire
October 1993

Zoe Bacharach: '*Nice Girls* documented the story of the occupation of Trentham Colliery by the North Staffordshire Miners' Wives Action Group, in protest against its threatened closure in 1993.

'Act I developed into small, domestic scenes requiring tables, chairs and benches. Act II dramatised the break-in and occupation of the pit and needed a hostile, industrial environment. Our theatre-in-the-round was the ideal spatial environment because it increased the involvement of the audience, drawing them into small, intimate scenes.

'Using the open space above the stage enhanced the difference in size between the women and the huge machinery of the pit.'

Director: Peter Cheeseman
Designer: Zoe Bacharach
Lighting designer: Paul Jones
Photo credit: Robert Day

PURPOSE-BUILT ADAPTABLE SPACES

The rash of repertory theatres built in the 1960s and 70s and designed as flexible spaces present a contradiction. On the one hand they encourage the habit of going to the theatre in a familiar, friendly building, on the other they deliberately provoke the frisson of the unexpected inside the auditorium. Based on the premise that different productions require different spaces, many of the examples in this section are about creating an appropriately shaped playing area. Studio spaces often create a world in which the show can take place. While these theatre formats seem to encourage the impression that we are all in one big room, images are often presented out of black; only occasionally does the studio present productions in laboratory conditions, exposing the room to its occupants.

OCTAGON THEATRE

Bolton
1967

The Octagon was the first theatre to be built in the North West after the war, and the first in the country with a purpose-built adaptable space.

The auditorium construction is an elongated octagon within the (paradoxically) hexagonal super-structure. It has one permanent seating block with additional movable seating 'bleachers' which are used to create the various stage formats: end-stage, thrust, large and small round, semi-promenade, music hall and traverse. The seating is regularly adapted: the 1993/94 season used five different formats with change-overs implemented seven times during the season.

A 2.1m wide 'shelf' forms a perimeter walkway at 2.59m above the stage floor. It is a permanent concrete structure and inevitably dictates the dynamics of the space. It cuts into the back of the 'stage' for end-stage, thrust and semi-promenade formats and is therefore challenging to work round.

Above all, the Octagon is an intimate space. The maximum distance from the stage is nine rows (end-stage) with the median for all formats being six rows.

Autumn 1994 saw the opening of a second auditorium – the Bill Naughton Theatre, which is a fully adaptable 'black' box with a maximum capacity of 100.

Architects: Jack Bogle, EGS Design and Bolton Council Architects Department

THIS IMAGE HAS BEEN SPONSORED BY THE OCTAGON THEATRE, BOLTON

DERBY DAY ▶

Bill Naughton, adapted by Lawrence Till

Octagon Theatre, Bolton,
May 1994

Richard Foxton: 'We adapted the theatre for traverse (not one of its usual formats), so I had some say in designing the stage space. Terraced houses ran across both ends of the traverse with members of the audience in the upstairs windows (twitching the curtains). Other audience members sat on stone steps around the front of the two main seating blocks at the sides of the stage.'

Director: Lawrence Till
Designer: Richard Foxton
Lighting designer: Jeremy Newman Roberts
Choreographer: Lorelei Lynn

▲
Cabaret

Masteroff, Kander and Ebb,
after Christopher Isherwood

**Octagon Theatre, Bolton
September 1993**

Ashley Shairp: 'With the Octagon in its very open promenade format it was obvious to Ian Forrest and me that we should transform the whole space into the atmosphere and world of the Kit Kat Club.

'With a circular central stage, surrounded by an audience seated at tables, we placed the band above on the theatre's natural shelf. Underneath this we created a seedy, tatty Blue Angel-esque world where the club's boys and girls could sit, read, screw, apply their make-up, and be ready to drag furniture and props up on to the main disc.'

Director: Ian Forrest
Designer: Ashley Shairp
Lighting designer: Jeremy Newman Roberts
Choreographer: Lorelei Lynn

SLAUGHTER HOUSE 5

Adapted by Vince Foxhall and Paddy Cuneen

Liverpool Everyman, June 1990

Paul Kondras: '*Slaughter House 5* is an epic tale that rambles from 1960s, Midwest America to the destruction of Dresden in 1945, via the planet Trafalmador. Prisoner of war camps, pornographic bookshops, hospitals – almost every page was a different location. The set contained all the elements needed to propel the audience along as swiftly as the script demanded. It was littered with fragments of fuselage from a Flying Fortress complete with Varga girl, mountains of unsold science fiction novels by Kilgore Trout and thousands of pieces of broken china. The major scene change occurred when the audience put on 3D glasses in true 1950s style.'

Director: Paddy Cuneen
Designer: Paul Kondras
Lighting designer: Mo Hemming

INDIA SONG

Marguerite Duras

Theatr Clwyd Studio, September 1993

Directors: Annie Castledine and Annabel Arden
Designer: Iona McLeish
Lighting designer: Paule Constable
Choreographer: Wendy Allnutt

DRACULA

Liz Lockhead

The Arts Educational School, June 1994

Anouk Emanuel: 'I wanted to use the power of the circle to suggest the layers in this surprisingly complex melodrama – Stoneyfields within Bedlam, within Dracula's castle. To avoid the proscenium cutting into the set and diminishing the encircling effect, the stage was extended into the auditorium and the design was brought forward of the proscenium. The empty upstage space accentuated the scale of the Ernst-like petrified trees and 'moon.' Cloudscapes, front-projected on to the back-lit cyclorama, allowed powerful changes of mood from the English summer country garden to a grisly Bedlam and stormy, wolf-wailing castles.'

Director: John Perry
Designer: Anouk Emanuel
Lighting designer: Di Steadman

ALADDIN

Ian Cullen

Elmhurst Studio Theatre, Surrey
Elmhurst Ballet School, November 1993

Alan Schofield: 'Traditionally painted backcloths form the core of pantomime scenery, creating spaces which cannot exist in any other form. Inspired by the works of Sandro del Prete, Bruno Ernst and MC Escher, I painted just such an impossible space for Abanazar's lair.'

Director: Peta Fry
Set designer: Alan Schofield
Costume designer: Jane Webb
Lighting designer: Nigel Longley
Choreographer: Mercia Hetherington

OUR COUNTRY'S GOOD

Timberlake Wertenbaker

St Mary's College Theatre, London
Department of Drama, May 1991

Haibo Yu: 'The play opens on a convict ship bound for Australia, in 1787. A great sail rises above the parched colour of the floor where an 18th-century map design suggests the hardships of ocean navigation. On land, officers' quarters become prisoners' confines, with the exchange of an elegant and incongruous chair for a few sea-stained packing cases and a length of heavy chain. Canvas tent doors sometimes lead inwards to the intimacy of an officer with his prayer book, sometimes outwards to the bush or a sea-shore.'

Director: Elizabeth Byrne Hill
Set designer: Haibo Yu

THE GATE THEATRE

Notting Hill, London
Redesigned 1993

Tim Foster: 'The expansion of the Gate increases the seating capacity from 56 to 132 and significantly improves the foyer, dressing rooms and technical facilities. The enlargement of the auditorium involved removing almost all of the internal structural walls. There is now a fully equipped control room and lighting grid. Sound proofing has been improved and air conditioning installed. The space is larger, but retains the character and intimacy of the old theatre. The seating can be arranged in two principal formats: an end-stage or a traverse-stage, although there are variations.'

Architects: Tim Foster Architects
Photo credit: John Edward Linden

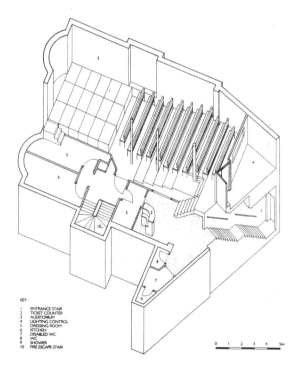

KEY
1   ENTRANCE STAIR
2   TICKET COUNTER
3   AUDITORIUM
4   LIGHTING CONTROL
5   DRESSING ROOM
6   KITCHEN
7   DISABLED WC
8   WC
9   SHOWER
10 FIRE ESCAPE STAIR

0 1 2 3 4 5m

THE MARQUIS OF KEITH
Frank Wedekind

**The Gate Theatre, Notting Hill, London
September 1991**

Claudia Mayer: 'Before renovation, the Gate was an awkward, low-ceilinged, irregular, tiny space. It was also wonderfully idiosyncratic and infinitely malleable.

'In this Faustian tale of ends and means, the sexy, bullying, swindling Marquis aims to build a Palace of the Arts in pre-First World War Munich. I wanted to represent a world of claustrophobia, of duplicity and traps. I decided to cut the space up, creating smaller and hidden areas using screens and hangings. The Marquis' study was approached down a long corridor, thrusting the actors towards the audience and their fate, crammed aboard their ship of fools.'

Director: Mark Dornford-May
Designer: Claudia Mayer
Lighting designer: Charles Balfour
Photo credit: Simon Annand

BOHEMIAN LIGHTS
Ramon Maria Valle d'Inclan

**The Gate Theatre, Notting Hill, London
July 1993**

Ace McCarron: 'Richard Hudson's set proposals had been described as almost completely light-proof. The entire lighting budget was reallocated to the wardrobe department. The wake scene had 18 actors blocked into a space 3m by 1.5m with two folding chairs and a coffin. Half the Fresnels and Parcans had disappeared during the building work. However, the new air conditioning worked perfectly, nobody was seriously injured and the lighting design was nominated for a London Fringe Award.'

Director: Lawrence Boswell
Set designer: Richard Hudson
Costume designer: Rosa Maggiora
Lighting designer: Ace McCarron

SWEENEY TODD

Stephen Sondheim

Cottesloe Theatre
Royal National Theatre, June 1993

Nick Ormerod: 'The complex technical requirements of the piece – trap doors, chutes and so on – are contained within a mobile bridge. Its mobility allows the use of a bare stage on which the actors themselves propel the relatively simple scenic elements such as doors and tables. Costume alone suggests the sense of period.'

Director: Declan Donnellan
Designer: Nick Ormerod
Lighting designer: Mick Hughes
Director of movement: Jane Gibson
Music director: Paddy Cunneen
Photo credit: John Haynes

THE SKRIKER

Caryl Churchill and Judith Weir

Cottesloe Theatre
Royal National Theatre, January 1994

Annie Smart: 'The Skriker is a fairy monster who transforms herself 13 times while pursuing two young girls. The play is a collection of modern day fairy stories and transformations, a collaborative, multi-disciplined theatre event involving 16 actors, dancers and singers and four musicians and was presented in the National Theatre's smallest performance space.'

Director: Les Waters
Designer: Annie Smart
Lighting designer: Christopher Toulmin
Choreographer: Ian Spink
Photo credit: Jörg Marohn

I TOO SPEAK OF THE ROSE
Emilio Carballido

The Brickhouse Studio, Contact Theatre, Manchester, May 1993

Andrew Wood: 'The need for a fixed environment of a rubbish dump and a more open, adaptable area for other locations and slide projections led the staging into a form of traverse. The railway tracks provided a physical link between the two areas and a course for journeys, as well as being integral to the action of the play. The dump itself was to provide a home for society's lowest, while also being a percussion instrument within the original music.'

Director: Renny O Shea
Designer: Andrew Wood
Lighting designer: Jack Lloyd and Chris Brockhouse
Composer: Olly Fox

CLOUD NINE
Caryl Churchill

Contact Theatre, Manchester, May 1992

Janey Gardiner: '*Cloud Nine* is initially set in a 19th-century, colonial context and examines racism, sexism and sexual hypocrisy. Act II brings certain characters up to date (1970s) and looks at their self-development in the context of the modern world. In Act I the architectural structure and the actors within it, becomes a museum exhibit of Victoriana surrounded by poles and ropes and crowned by a British Standard. Act II sees the structure stripped back to become a piece of park architecture with brightly coloured panels and flooring. Throughout the play the key relationship is that between the open space of the thrust, marked to represent the grounds, and the structure behind.'

Director: Burt Caesar
Designer: Janey Gardiner
Lighting designer: Chris Brockhouse

THE THREEPENNY OPERA
Bertolt Brecht and Kurt Weill

Contact Theatre, Manchester, April 1994

Simon Banham: 'This was designed to explore the full extent of the performance space in each dimension encompassing the dock doors, stage access doors and the fly floor. This created a charged open space within which objects became specific and the distance between performers was a tangible presence.'

Director: Annie Castledine
Designer: Simon Banham
Lighting designer: Nick Beadle
Choreographer: Josette Bushel-Mingo
Musical director: Tony Castro

THE YOUNG VIC

London

Refurbished in 1993

Christopher Richardson: 'In a sense, the last place to put on a play is in a theatre. A corridor or a cupboard may serve the purpose. The black box allows flexibility but may depress the audience. The galleried proscenium provides a sense of occasion but may inhibit new ideas.

'John Partridge's brilliant "courtyard" at The Young Vic packs people near to the action and encourages experiment. The present refurbishment eases the change from one form to another. It subdues the balcony rail which, though fun and jolly, foiled attempts to focus on the action as it glowed, a vibrant circle of red, in unfair competition with the designer's efforts. The Young Vic was and I hope still is, a classic and may explain why there can be no consensus as to what best constitutes a theatre.'

Theatre consultants: Theatre Futures
Designer: Christopher Richardson
Set design in this image: Ashley Martin-Davies
THIS IMAGE HAS BEEN SPONSORED BY THEATRE FUTURES

SILVERLANDS ▶
Antoine O'Flatharta

Peacock Theatre, Dublin
Abbey Theatre Company, 1992

Francis O'Connor: '*Silverlands* was a new play set in a nightclub in a small town in Ireland. It made many different demands on the design which had to allow for several different spaces to exist: by the bar, the toilets, the street outside and the dance floor. The set was originally more complex than this but paring the design down to just bar stools, thrusting through a blue, raked floor and shards of mirror, freed the space into a disco landscape. At the end of the play there is a killing. Just lighting the tops of the bar stools created an image of drops of blood suspended in space.'

Director: Andy Hinds
Designer: Francis O Connor
Lighting designer: Rupert Murray
Photo credit: Colman Corish

BRIGHTON ROCK

Graham Greene, adapted by John Elliott

Seagull Theatre, Lowestoft, May 1994

Ian Westbrook: 'There are two themes in this play: the first, light-hearted, candy-floss weekends by the sea; the second, more sinister, illustrating Brighton's criminal underworld. The space was very limiting. We had no facility for flying scenery, no wing space, just a basic box 7m by 7m by 4.2m height to the grid. The show requires ten scene locations, internal and external, with a cast of 30 and an on-stage band of five musicians, demanding fast and silent changes of scene.'

Director: Patrick Redsell
Set designer: Ian Westbrook
Costume designers: Ian Westbrook and Christeen Grimmer
Lighting designer: Jim Laws
Photo credit: William Goodman

KING BABY

James Robson

The Pit, Barbican Centre, London
Royal Shakespeare Company, January 1993

Anthony Lamble: 'The Pit is an epic, three-sided venue, more suited to classic drama than to the detailed realism of *King Baby*. We used the upstage wall to maximum effect, concentrating a lot of the necessary detail here. A raked floor improved sight lines while a sloping, suspended ceiling implied the confinement of the attic. The effect is one of religious tranquillity, a real room in which people hope for change.'

Director: Simon Usher
Designer: Anthony Lamble
Lighting designer: Ace McCarron

THIS IMAGE HAS BEEN SPONSORED BY KEN FLEARY AND MATTHEW SCOTT OF SCOTT FLEARY LTD

ALL'S WELL THAT ENDS WELL

William Shakespeare

Arden School of Theatre Studio, Manchester, July 1993

Carla Eve Amie: 'The director and I wanted to create a space that conveyed the wonder and complexity of growing up and reaching out to the unknown. Familiar blankets and sheets covered the floor and windows; fabrics formed children's clothes; hair, thread and stuffing pulled up from the floor, twisted and grew into a matted rope which shot off diagonally across the space, over the audience's head and quite literally off into the outside world. The correctness in costume style (late 1930s) heightened the organic nature of the set.'

Director: Richard Brandon
Designer: Carla Eve Amie
Lighting designer: Helen McGuire

THE ABDUCTION

Hilary Westlake

ICA, London
Lumiere & Son, November 1992

Sanja Jurca: 'The play required three rooms which inhabited the stage simultaneously. These needed intimacy and at the same time accessibility for the omnipresent Strangers' characters. When the Strangers visited, the whole space took on an eerie atmosphere created by the bacilli-like, fluorescent lights which were an integral part of the set design.'

Director: Hilary Westlake
Designer: Sanja Jurca
Lighting designer: Simon Corder
Music: Jeremy Peyton-Jones
Photo credit: Miha Dobrin

THRUST AND OPEN STAGES

Arguably the most difficult format for set and lighting designers, the thrust stage is a legacy from the theatre of the first Elizabethan age. There are few purpose-built theatres with a complete thrust stage in this country (they include the Festival Theatre in Chichester, the Crucible in Sheffield and the Swan Stratford upon Avon), but it is a format often also used in a in adaptable spaces. Generally the thrust becomes the main acting area because of its close proximity to the whole audience. The floor becomes an important design feature, relegating scenic information to the upstage area. By creating strong diagonals, both scenically and dramatically (which may also extend into the auditorium) the two areas can be drawn together to create a powerful dynamic throughout the theatre space. Lighting designers may well ponder on the fact that Elizabethan theatres played in daylight hours and that there was only the angle of the sun to dazzle the audience's eyes.

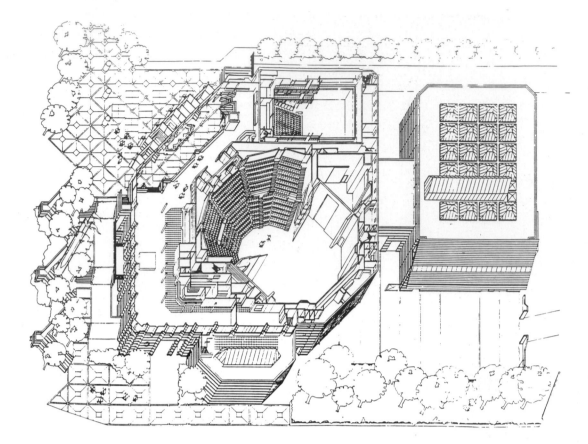

WEST YORKSHIRE PLAYHOUSE

Leeds, 1990

Ian Appleton: 'Theatre architecture is a fusion between often disparate interests and requirements, a search for the controlling order that underlines the geometry of a building to produce a recognisable image both externally and internally.

'Ultimately though, the building is a backdrop to the intense activity of putting on a play in a scenic environment to an expectant audience. The Quarry Theatre, the larger of the two auditoria, provides seating for 750 on a single, steep rake establishing a cohesion of the audience, good sightlines and above all the performers' command of the audience.

'During the briefing, artistic director John Harrison stressed that the audience should cluster around the stage, as though it were a booth theatre, with seating rows faceted to provide an angular, rather than curved, geometry. We have created an intimate space with the audience embracing the stage. While acknowledging the Greco-Roman amphitheatre, the form of The Quarry is unique and builds on the successful open-stage presentation style developed in the old Leeds Playhouse.

'The Courtyard Theatre, the second auditorium, bears more than a nodding resemblance to the Georgian theatre in nearby Richmond. This auditorium does not follow the studio tradition, nor is it a neutral black box. With a seating capacity of up to 350 and a level of flexibility, it allows for various configurations including end-stage, theatre-in-the-round and promenade. The public area – the bar and restaurant – is, in effect, a third performance space suitable for a range of small-scale performances.'

Architects: The Appleton Partnership
Artistic Director: Jude Kelly

WILD OATS ▶
John O'Keefe

The Quarry Theatre, West Yorkshire Playhouse
March 1990

Robert Jones: 'This was the opening production in the new Quarry Theatre. No one had ever designed for the space before, so my approach to it was unique; I had no guidelines to follow but this was one of my most instinctive designs. Standing with my director, production manager and the architects in an empty auditorium with no seats, trying to understand the stage and all its focal points, was not easy.

'*Wild Oats* is a celebration of theatre in the mid-18th century and as such we decided to approach the production along those lines. It was also the celebration of a new theatre space and I therefore incorporated as many dynamics of the space as possible: flying pieces, traps set with furniture rising up from below, walls sliding diagonally across the space to divide it and large moving drapes to add a theatrical sweep.'

Director: Jude Kelly
Designer: Robert Jones
Lighting designer: Jenny Cane
Music: Chris Marks

BRIGHTON ROCK

Graham Greene, adapted by David Horlock

**The Quarry Theatre, West Yorkshire Playhouse
October 1993**

Ken Coker: 'The look and feel of this production were inspired by the works of John Piper and in particular his Brighton Aquatints, published the year after Greene's novel. Light, shade and shadow play an important part in Greene's Brighton: the tall Regency buildings with their stucco walls at one moment reflecting light and the next creating shadow; the light under the pier with the darkness created by the planking and the bracing. Most important is the darkness of the district where Pinkie lives - the small, tightly packed houses causing areas of almost permanent shadow.

'It was some of Piper's other work that defined the broad washes of colour – particularly his Coventry Cathedral and Royal Holloway College. I also wanted to represent the atmosphere of Brighton on a Bank Holiday and to try and draw people's minds away from the images in the film that everyone remembers.'

Director: Jude Kelly
Designer: Kate Burnett
Lighting designer: Ken Coker

SAVAGES

Christopher Hampton

**The Quarry Theatre, West Yorkshire Playhouse
September 1991**

Saul Radomsky: 'This was conceived as a composite set showing living room, mission station, hostage cell, veranda and rain forest. One of the advantages of this production was the addition of 50 extras from the Theatre Club. Making these natives of Leeds look, act, dance and chant like the natives of Brazil was challenging and in the end very successful.'

Director: Jude Kelly
Designer: Saul Radomsky
Lighting designer: Michael Calf
Photo credit: Jill Furmanovsky

GYPSY

Jule Styne and Stephen Sondheim

**The Quarry Theatre, West Yorkshire Playhouse
December 1993**

Paul Andrews: 'We created the world of the stripper Gypsy Rose Lee and her influential stage mother, depicting the harsh reality of the American Depression without robbing the musical of its scenic treats. The orchestra was incorporated into the set, appearing and disappearing at the back.'

Director: Jude Kelly
Designer: Paul Andrews
Lighting designer: Michael Calf

SHE STOOPS TO CONQUER
Oliver Goldsmith

Newcastle Playhouse
Northern Stage, October 1993

Neil Murray: 'A monochrome, 18th-century playhouse was created in the 1976 Playhouse auditorium. Changes of location were created through the misuse of traditional theatre technique. An opera box became the area of a boudoir; a front cloth, half lowered, became the ceiling of a pub and was then further lowered to become a garden wall. All furniture and decorative elements had an obvious two-dimensional, engraved quality about them, without the cross-hatching.'

Director/designer: Neil Murray
Lighting designer: Dave Lovett
Photo credit: Keith Pattison

DEATH OF A SALESMAN
Arthur Miller

Pitlochry Festival Theatre, 1992 season

Trevor Coe: 'A traditional, American, whitewashed, clapboard house, squeezed between modern apartment blocks which are dwarfing the Loman family home. A large part of this play happens in Willy Loman's mind, as flashbacks and so a thin, unreal quality was required. As in the original production, gauze was used on the walls. The apartments were effected by stripping out the theatre's masking and painting the walls and bolting light-box windows in horizontal rows. The apartment windows could then transform and bleed through the walls giving us control over the degree of solidity of the house. As is usual in Pitlochry, the single biggest design and technical problem was in overcoming the two hour turnaround of our six-show repertoire.'

Director: Clive Perry
Set designer: Trevor Coe
Costume designer: Helen Wilkinson
Lighting designer: Kevin Sleep

AN IDEAL HUSBAND

Oscar Wilde

Pitlochry Festival Theatre, April 1994

Edward Lipscomb: 'I wanted to suggest a world in which the characters were marooned in a sea of constraints imposed by Victorian convention and morality.

'The play was enacted on a steeply raked marquetry octagon. Echoing the floor, a vast gold-encrusted ceiling, with painted panel depicting 'The Triumph of Love', loomed overhead.'

Director: Clive Perry
Set designer: Edward Lipscomb
Costume designer: Alexander Reid
Lighting designer: Kevin Sleep
Photo credit: Sean Hudson

THE GRAPES OF WRATH

John Steinbeck, adapted by Frank Galati

Crucible Theatre, Sheffield
February 1994

Peter Ruthven Hall: 'The Joad family – farmers dispossessed of their livelihood – head west across the parched American wilderness towards a promised land of orange trees and full employment. Set on a thrust stage with virtually no wing space or capacity for flying scenery, the basic set had to accommodate a cinematic journey through 22 scenes without a break in the action. The bone-shaker truck holding 13 people and all their belongings turned on its pivot between scenes to help establish different locales. It was important to position the vehicle sufficiently far downstage to facilitate playing intimate scenes on or in it, whilst also allowing sufficient acting space around it and without masking the action from the side audience.'

Director: Michael Rudman
Designer: Peter Ruthven Hall
Lighting designer: Gerry Jenkinson

LA VIE DE BOHÈME

Henri Mürger, adapted by John Clifford

Pitlochry Festival Theatre, August 1993

Ken Harrison. 'John Clifford's play points up the ironies of Henri Mürger's original account of Bohemian life, where ideals are eroded by market forces as Rodolphe finally sells Mimi's story to survive. In this composite set, the floor of the garret doubles as a cabaret stage.'

Director: Clive Perry
Designer: Ken Harrison
Lighting designer: Kevin Sleep
Photo credit: Sean Hudson

THE SNOW QUEEN

Mike Kenny

Sherman Theatre, Cardiff, November 1993

Jane Linz Roberts: 'Four children break into an old house. Tall, frosted windows, across which shadows flicker, allow wintry light to seep into the dark interior. A story within a story needs a theatre within a theatre, a circle within a circle.

'A woman ascends a staircase from the orchestra pit "downstairs". Looking into the circular mirror overhead, she begins...heavy drapes peel away, releasing the space...furniture transforms into land-scape...the circle revolves to animate journeys... blossom transforms into snow...going north to where there are no people. Translucency reveals the Snow Queen, filling the space, with light bouncing off shards of mirror. Windows become pillars of ice. Her destruction restores the house – full circle.'

Director: Phil Clark
Designer: Jane Linz Roberts
Lighting designer: Nick MacLiammoir
Musical director: Matthew Bailey

THIS IMAGE HAS BEEN SPONSORED BY STAGEWORKS

BILLY LIAR

Keith Waterhouse and Willis Hall

Salisbury Playhouse, August 1993

Jonathan Fensom: 'Set in the north of England, the Fishers' suburban street was represented by three flown bay windows, complete with net curtains and flying ducks. By getting rid of the walls we were able to leave the room open to the sky and create an island on which we could evoke the stark cosiness of a 1950s home.'

Director: David Massarella
Designer: Jonathan Fensom
Lighting designer: Peter Hunter

MACBETH

William Shakespeare

Sherman Theatre, Cardiff, February 1994

Jane Linz Roberts: 'Moving fluidly from the epic to the intimate in the large, space-precise focus of a close-up, alongside big austere shapes suggesting a beyond. Open space releases the energy of a sport. Diagonal tunnels steer strong entrances spilling light and shadows. In the light there is detail, outside the light a sketch. Shapes of the walls, part of a circle on the floor imply a space which completes in the imagination of the audience, in their space. Two worlds: Christian – right and wrong; magical – wanting and making things happen. Falling walls, the destruction of fire and water.'

Director: Jamie Garven
Designer: Jane Linz Roberts
Lighting designer: Nick MacLiammoir
Musical director: Matthew Bailey

THESE IMAGES HAS BEEN SPONSORED BY STAGEWORKS AND SPECIALIST LAMPS

THE THREE SISTERS

Anton Chekov

Wolsey Theatre, Ipswich
October 1991

David Knapman: 'Using the full depth of the Wolsey stage, nearly 14 metres, the basic set was a wooden, chevron-panelled box with doorways and entrances concealed until required, with a matching false floor, wood-dyed in reds and golds and browns. Acts I and II were fully dressed with a flown back wall section hung with family photographs. Act III was played downstage with only furniture as dressing to realise the bedroom. Autumn leaves softened the floor for Act IV.'

Director: Hettie MacDonald
Designer: David Knapman
Lighting designer: Geoff Spain
Photo credit: Mike Kwasniak

THESE IMAGES HAVE BEEN SPONSORED BY THE WOLSEY THEATRE, IPSWICH

A DOLL'S HOUSE

Henrik Ibsen

Wolsey Theatre, Ipswich, May 1992

Marjoke Henrichs: 'We wanted to create the feel of a spacious Scandinavian mansion flat, on an upper floor, with many rooms but no windows. The Wolsey Theatre is hexagonal, has no flying, no wing space and has a small scene dock at the back. There are balconies supported by pillars all the way round the stage area. I used the height of these balconies as the set ceiling and created the same image above them. I used all the space possible going to the far wall at the back and to the sides under the balconies into the storage areas, making rooms which all connected with each other. You could see glimpses of the other interiors from any sightline up to the main stairwell behind the front door.'

Director: Hettie MacDonald
Designer: Marjoke Henrichs
Lighting designer: Geoff Spain
Photo credit: Mike Kwasniak

◄ NO MAN'S LAND

Harold Pinter

Wolsey Theatre, Ipswich, October 1993

David Knapman: 'A red room with a gentle, carpeted rake receded to the only doorway. The walls and ceiling were covered in display felt and then had mouldings added so that no joins were visible. All dressings and props were black and red. The costumes were in shades of grey going into black.'

Director: Antony Tuckey
Designer: David Knapman
Lighting designer: Geoff Spain
Photo credit: Mike Kwasniak

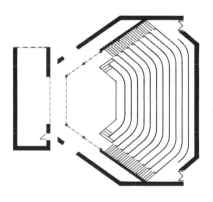

WOLSEY THEATRE

Ipswich, Suffolk

David Knapman: 'The Wolsey Theatre, seating 400 people, opened in 1979. It incorporates a large thrust stage with side galleries three metres high and supported by pillars. These galleries can be joined by a movable bridge which can only be winched in manually. When in position the building takes on the appearance of a modern Elizabethan stage. The theatre has no flying facilities and only limited wing space. Over the years we have included a false stage with its own revolve and, in the basement, a plant to power below-stage hydraulics. At present we produce 12 main-house productions a year and four studio productions and have a thriving theatre-in-education company.'

Architect: Roderick Ham and Partners
Head of design: David Knapman
Artistic director: Antony Tuckey

THE BEGGAR'S OPERA

John Gay

The Swan Theatre, Stratford-Upon-Avon
Royal Shakespeare Company, April 1992

Kendra Ullyart: 'My aim was to capture the atmosphere of the shadowy underworld of the beggar classes in 1728.

'Two balconies on insubstantial supports were built on to the thrust stage area, the extensions sagging dangerously. Makeshift staircases were lashed on with fraying rope. Sagging shelves, full of old props, were used to break up the clean lines of the galleries. The overall impression was of a theatre, built by the beggars themselves, which could collapse at any moment.

'The transfer to the modern proscenium Barbican Theatre necessitated a rethink. Practically and aesthetically the sagging balconies had no auditorium to link on to, but, still excited by the atmosphere of danger created with the Swan set, I designed a condemned opera house on stage. On its sunken floor and between its crumbling walls, the original set was recreated to span the opera house boxes and extend to the front of the new "proscenium arch". This created some degree of the audience-stage relationship as at the Swan and generated the impression that the beggars had spilled out from their own stage and were in the auditorium, with the audience.'

Director: John Caird
Designer: Kendra Ullyart
Lighting designer: David Hersey
Music: Ilona Sekacz
Photo credit: Donald Cooper

THESE IMAGES HAVE BEEN SPONSORED BY THE ROYAL SHAKESPEARE COMPANY

"ROBIN OF BAGSHOT"

BEGGARS OPERA "NIMMING NED" - ULLYART 92 - RSC.

GARS OPERA ~ SUKY TAWDRY ~ ULTYART RSC 92

THE THEBANS
— Antigone, Oedipus Tyrannos and Oedipus at Colonnus

Sophocles, translated by Timberlake Wertenbaker

The Swan Theatre, Stratford-Upon-Avon
Royal Shakespeare Company, November 1991

Ultz: 'Early on we thought of staging *The Thebans* in-the-round, of putting a stage across the whole Swan, but because we were going to perform in repertoire we couldn't do that. Still, we knew we needed a more formal staging than the Swan is normally and to find a style that is a true contract between actor and audience.

'We had a good upstage entrance, but there was nowhere to go when you got downstage apart from one emergency exit at stage level: we put a formal walkway there. This seemed to us to be a parallel to the entrance of the Chorus in Greek drama, the 'parados'.

'Secondly, the plays were debating issues of interest to the audience of the time. We had to set up a formal debating platform. The Swan is wonderful as a court of law: the jury either side and the defence and prosecution in the centre. We moved some of the side seating and put the Chorus, at times, in a privileged audience position, formally placed so that there would be a dignity in their response to the protagonists.'

Director: Adrian Noble
Designer: Ultz
Lighting designer: Alan Burrett
Photo credit: Donald Cooper

THESE IMAGES HAVE BEEN SPONSORED BY THE ROYAL SHAKESPEARE COMPANY

AN INSPECTOR CALLS

J B Priestley

Olivier Theatre, Royal National Theatre
September 1992

Rick Fisher: 'When reminded that a public confession is required, the Inspector ushers in a group of witnesses from the play's present to hear of the family's responsibility. The skyscape changes from stormy blue to an ominous yellow as a crowd enters from the distance – their shadows forcing the Birling family to cower in a downstage corner as they wait to hear the truth of their own guilt.'

Director: Stephen Daldry
Designer: Ian MacNeil
Lighting designer: Rick Fisher
Composer: Stephen Warbeck
Photo credit: Ivan Kyncl

CORIOLANUS

William Shakespeare

Shaw Theatre, Stratford-upon-Avon
Royal Shakespeare Company, May 1994

Fran Thompson: 'The French Revolution seemed an appropriate setting for the reinvention of the Roman Republic of Coriolanus. The setting is broadly Naploeonic and the costumes and props Empire. The Swan Theatre is an exacting space. The dramatic strength of the building lies in its vertical height, the runway of the stage and proximity of the wraparound audience. These are elements I tried to exploit in an environmental design.'

Director: David Thacker
Set designer: Fran Thompson
Lighting designer: Alan Burrett
Movement: Adrian Hutchinson
Music: Adrian Johnstone
Photo credit: Alastair Muir

THIS IMAGE HAS BEEN SPONSORED BY CENTRAL SCHOOL OF SPEECH AND DRAMA

PROSCENIUM THEATRES

The familiarity and focus of the proscenium frames the human figure. It places it in proportion to the scenic elements and to the frame itself. Whether two or three dimensional, these elements operate within the convention of a picture and create perspectives in which a foreground, mid-ground and background can be understood, again, in relation to the figure. The provocative element of proscenium theatres is the line between stage and audience. Music hall and vaudeville use it to tease and strut; architectural and domestic sets use it as the edge between different worlds. The frame, ornate and historic or bleak and contemporary, presents the show to the audience. It is artifice plainly stated. The task in hand, whether it is to reach out into the audience, to suggest other worlds or barely to contain momentous events, is to enable the action to proceed without the pretence that they are one of us or vice versa. So the imagination crosses over in both directions.

MACHINAL

Sophie Treadwell

Lyttleton Theatre, Royal National Theatre
October 1993

Rick Fisher: 'The ceiling lowers to create a lovers' nest (right), but first they climb out and feel the expansive joy of freedom. A heavily coloured scene in contrast to most of the play – deep blue shot through with gold and pastels emphasises the first romance and happiness in the play.

'Buried beneath the workings of the Lyttleton stage, the electric chair rises into view. The audience can just barely see the woman through the mechanics and structure of the stage. Dimly lit and horribly rendered by the glare of arc welding, the smoke becomes a rainbow symbolising the young woman's final release.'

Director: Stephen Daldry
Set designer: Ian MacNeil
Costume designer: Clare Mitchell
Lighting designer: Rick Fisher
Choreographer: Quinny Sacks
Composer: Stephen Warbeck
Photo credit: Ivan Kyncl

HAMLET

William Shakespeare

Bloomsbury Theatre, London
Triumvirate Productions, November 1992

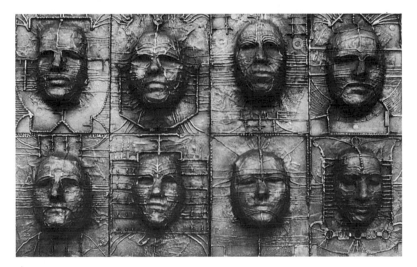

David B Palser: 'The direction and choreography of this production were treated in a very film-like manner. I designed *Hamlet* in a way that resembled a cinematic, wide-screen format by changing the proportions of the proscenium arch. The concept was that Elsinore had become a militaristic outpost full of ever-watchful eyes and distorted reflections. The exterior/battlement scenes involved harsh beams of cross-light, evocative of searchlights, which played across the blasted metal bulkheads representing the castle walls.

'The detailed columns, which were to form a major part of the setting, had to be both beautiful and sinister. The fusion of recognisably human faces with hard industrial forms evoked an air of suppression and imprisonment, indicative of the society living within the walls of Elsinore. Since the 5.5m columns had to truck in and out as well as fly, they had to be constructed from fairly light materials. Plaster casts were made of the actors' faces and set in glue. Detailing was added and then they were brushed up to a graphite finish. Mood changes were achieved by a combination of cross- and under-lighting.'

Director: Alexander Wood
Designer: David B Palser
Lighting designer: Andrew Strickland

THE KITCHEN
Arnold Wesker

Royal Court, London
February 1994

Mark Thompson: 'The task here was to develop an environment in which the apparent chaos of the commercial kitchen could be fully experienced by the audience. By pushing the acting area over the stalls, the curve of the theatre circle dictated the overall shape of the acting space. What emerged was an arena around which the kitchen staff could battle. The shape of the proscenium arch, clad in white tiles, informed the position of any walls and doors. The result was a clash of opposites: the gilt and plush of a theatre embracing the grime and steel of a kitchen.'

Director: Stephen Daldry
Designer: Mark Thompson
Lighting designer: Johanna Town
Photo credit: Ivan Kyncl

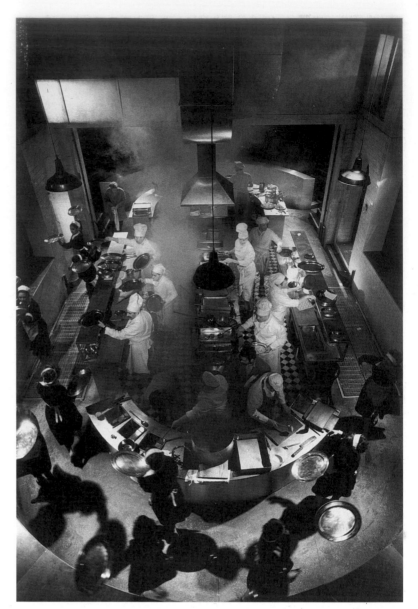

900 ONEONTA
David Beaird

Old Vic Theatre, London
Gero Productions, July 1994

Tim Shortall: 'The play shows a family in decay – its imminent downfall, spiritually, morally and materially brought about by self-consuming greed and decadence. This degeneration of one fabulously wealthy family in the Deep South, is, on a larger scale, a reflection of the demise of America. The concept behind the design was to suggest this deterioration from grandeur, through decay, to annihilation. The structure in a way is as crazy as the members of the family, lacking stability or verticals, no longer able to support itself, teetering on the brink of collapse, the vegetation forcing through the walls to the rotten heart of the house, and the nation.'

Director: David Beaird
Designer: Tim Shortall
Lighting designer: Howard Harrison
Photo credit: John Haynes

SAINT JOAN
George Bernard Shaw

Theatr Clwyd and Strand Theatre, London
Duncan C Weldon and Theatr Clwyd, May 1994

Peter J Davison: 'Saint Joan is a powerful rhetorical debate play set in seven distinct and disparate scenes, each of which must provide a special arena for Shaw's ideas. The concrete bunker – cold, impersonal and towering – became the metaphor for the male world of inflexible systems in which Joan speaks. Economy, simplicity and boldness were always the visual aims in the design. Rain, water, blue sky and stars were revealed and cruelly shut off by heavy sliding panels.'

Director: Gale Edward
Set designer: Peter J Davison
Costume designer: Clare Mitchell
Lighting designer: Mark Henderson

MOBY DICK – A WHALE OF A TALE
Robert Longden and Hereward Kaye

Piccadilly Theatre, London
Cameron Mackintosh Ltd, March 1992

Paul Farnsworth: 'The challenge here was to recreate, in a large proscenium theatre, the feeling of intimacy and anarchy that was an essential part of the production in its studio incarnation at the Old Fire Station, Oxford. The set reached into the auditorium on all levels - to the middle of the stalls, into the front of the circle and even into the roof, where bicycles and hockey sticks swayed over the heads of the audience. The entire prosc and anteprosc areas were painted and the prosc itself clad so that the actual structure was lost, while a false wall at the back of the upper circle made the auditorium feel more intimate.'

Director: Robert Longden
Set designer: Paul Farnsworth
Costume designer: Howard Rayner
Lighting designers: Andrew Bridge and Hugh Vanstone
Choreographer: Anthony Lapsley
Photo credit: Michael Le Poer Trench

MODEL VICTORIA THEATRE

Based on the Old Vic Theatre, London

Showing the set for the Magic Pool Scene in
Mother Goose

Tony Banfield: 'My most enduring childhood
memory is of a visit to the Lewisham Hippodrome,
a Frank Matcham confection of gold leaf and red
plush. I was hooked and from then on made a
succession of model theatres starting with an old
shoe-box. The Model Victoria Theatre is, I suppose,
the theatre I always wanted as a child but didn't
know how to make. It is based on the Old Vic
Theatre in 1871 and made at a scale of 1:25. There
are now ten versions, here and abroad, some with
full flying and lighting rigs, traps and revolves. Since
most of my work has been for non-traditional
spaces, I am pleased to be able to use the model to
show designs from a very traditional pantomime.'

Architect: J T Robinson, 1871
Set designer and model maker: Tony Banfield

MOTHER GOOSE

Theatre Royal, Windsor
December 1994

Tony Banfield: 'The frontcloth design is a visual
overture using themes and imagery from the story
and establishing the design style. I couldn't resist a
gentle send up of the Goose Ballet scene. The Imp
about to prod the dignity of the prima ballerina in
rehearsal could be me! As a painter I was interested
in exploring some of the scenic artist's tricks of
trompe l oeil. As you move around the picture the
rules of illusion and reality are always changing.'

Director: Hugh Goldie
Set designer: Tony Banfield
Costume designer: Marty Flood
Choreographer: Hazel Gee

THE ATHEIST'S TRAGEDY

Cyril Tourneur

Birmingham Repertory Theatre, February 1994

Patick Connellan: 'Spatially we wanted to use the vast width and depth of the stage to give the production an epic quality. The costumes were broadly modern (1950s) in order to make the characters, who spoke in an alienating way, more accessible.'

Tim Mitchell: 'Side beam lighting was used extensively, as the major element of the design comprised a faceted roof which ran from the auditorium, lighting bridges to two thirds of the stage depth. The use of strong colour and uplight was used to heighten the non-naturalism of the production.'

Director: Anthony Clarke
Designer: Patrick Connellan
Lighting designer: Tim Mitchell
Photo credit: Bob Wain

▼

▲

TRANSLATIONS

Brian Friel

Birmingham Repertory Theatre, April 1991

Tim Mitchell: 'The set for *Translations* had a roof and three curved cycloramas. This necessitated the use of unconventional lighting positions including three curved bars to light each cyc independently with strong colour. The acting area was lit through the roof and main doors with Svoboda light-curtains, giving a strong sense of directional light from outside. This was supplemented by a conventional rig over the main stage area. Night-time states were achieved by strong back lighting on the main cyc and the acting area was lit with one Svoboda light-curtain coloured in a two-colour split of steel grey and lavender to give parallel beams of moonlight.'

Ruari Murchison: 'Although *Translations* has a domestic setting we believed that there were epic qualities associated with the piece that needed to be reflected in the design. Oversized symbols became incorporated in the design. In turn the design cut down the huge opening of the Rep space in a way the audience did not notice, whilst an unfocused perspective allowed one to relate the height of the actors to a set that was over nine metres tall nearest to the audience.'

Director: Gwenda Hughes
Designer: Ruari Murchison
Lighting designer: Tim Mitchell

THE PIED PIPER

Anthony Clarke

Birmingham Repertory Theatre, December 1991

Patrick Connellan: 'The Piper leads the children into a mountain to teach their parents a lesson. We decided to give this a clear social context by setting the play in a decaying town with a corrupt council and a selfish divided populace. This became not only a mythical image of a rat-infested, peeling, gold castle but also a portrait of a society with strong modern parallels. Here amongst the rats and rubbish lived the children of the streets, very like the children of Bogatta. The front-cloth made of images of hundreds of photographs of the missing children of Hamlin resembled the 'disappeared' of South America. Scenically the circular walled town with its many secret doors was bisected by a number of flat images such as a massive pompous portrait of the mayor or a large, flat green hill with a small door to show the mountain into which the children were lured.'

Director: Anthony Clarke
Designer: Patrick Connellan
Lighting designer: Tim Mitchell
Composer: Mark Vibrans
Photo credit: Alan Wood

MY MOTHER SAID I NEVER SHOULD

Charlotte Keatley

Birmingham Repertory Theatre, February 1992

Fran Thompson: 'The time structure of the play is a complicated juxtaposition of past and present and another time, a dream-time, where all four characters meet and play as children. It was this dream-time that Tony and I wanted to explore to create a performance space that would heighten the expressionistic elements of the play.'

Director: Anthony Clarke
Designer: Fran Thompson
Lighting designer: Jenny Cane

ROMEO AND JULIET

William Shakespeare

Birmingham Repertory Theatre, October 1993

Robert Jones: 'This production gave us an opportunity to use the huge expanse of the space. As with many auditoria which are wider than the proscenium openings the sightlines determine a V-shaped acting space. We decided to capitalise on this by bringing the main floor through the proscenium by about four metres, thereby greatly increasing the best focal point.

'The actual set was a large open space, bordered by large architectural pieces which were covered by huge silk drapes. These followed the sightlines of the space and gave at the same time a feeling of intimacy or claustrophobia and great depth. In the final moments of the play when the drapes were removed and the ceiling piece lowered, we saw the full extent of the space surrounding the set, making the stage feel enormous and the actors small and vulnerable.'

Director: Gwenda Hughes
Designer: Robert Jones
Lighting designer: Tim Mitchell

OF MICE AND MEN

John Steinbeck

Birmingham Repertory Theatre
June 1990

Kate Burnett: 'The Birmingham Rep has a very wide and deep stage, but its sightlines allow only a shallow triangular playing area. The "little" human tragedy, *Of Mice and Men*, is played out against a rich evocation of nature and the cycle of day and night. Steinbeck's story is set in California – a land of milk and honey owned by someone else.

'This context was driven home by a vast roadside hoarding acting as the frontcloth. Nature and the time of day were formalised into three oblong shapes (one of which was the cyclorama) and a multi-coloured floor. Combinations of specified colours on the screens conjured up the essence of sunset on the riverbank, cornfields at midday and the huge night sky.

'Jenny Cane's lighting used the colours in the floor to answer those on the screens, emphasising the locations and times and yet also focusing on the actors in each environment. The almost two-dimensional scenic elements continued the march from back to front of the stage, while perspective telegraph poles drove diagonally across the stage. Their different proportions in relation to the characters were intended to help emphasise the hugeness of Lennie in the bunkhouse and in Crookes' Nativity crib-like room in the barn, while the height of the simple cut-out barn and the enormous curving branches on the riverbank made him the size of a child.'

Director: Anthony Clarke
Designer: Kate Burnett
Lighting designer: Jenny Cane

THE SOUND OF MUSIC

Rodgers and Hammerstein

Everyman Theatre, Cheltenham
March/April 1994

Michael E Hall: 'Nettie's simple balletic designs demand a similar approach to the lighting. The mirrored floor, which to the audience reflected the painted gauzes, also helped the sculpture of the space by uplighting the actors. Mirrored side panels, which would have continued the effect around the set, had to be cut due to construction problems. No time was available for a redesign or re-rigging so the side lighting never fulfilled what was intended.'

Director: Michael Houghton
Designer: Nettie Edwards
Lighting designer: Michael E Hall

THE WILD DUCK

Henrik Ibsen

Phoenix Theatre, London
The Peter Hall Company, May 1990

John and Elizabeth Bury: 'A realistic play, with a realistic production on a very conventional stage – but beneath the surface the emerging forces of the 20th-century theatre lie and are, we hope, reflected.'

Director: Sir Peter Hall
Design and lighting: John Bury
Costume design: John and Elizabeth Bury

MACBETH

William Shakespeare

Everyman Theatre, Cheltenham
October/November 1992

Michael E Hall: 'The lighting needed to create an atmosphere and mood rather than define the location. Steep backlight and low crosslight created spaces which stood out from the painted floor and gauze. These were lit separately to complete the picture. For other scenes, powerful footlights were used, lighting the actors and gauze as one. Electrical candles on the set were used as scenic elements rather than for trying to create fake candle light.'

Director: Michael Houghton
Designer: Nettie Edwards
Lighting designer: Michael E Hall

THESE IMAGES HAVE BEEN SPONSORED BY THE EVERYMAN THEATRE, CHELTENHAM

DESIGN FOR LIVING
Noel Coward

Everyman Theatre, Cheltenham
April 1991

Nettie Edwards: 'We wanted to make very specific emotional statements about each of the play's three spaces and the men who inhabit them. Practically, scene changes had to be done quickly and by a very small crew.

'Act I is set in an artist's studio in Paris – a long, low space right downstage and only 2.5 m deep. A hinged flat created the skylight ceiling and back wall. Most of the Act II furniture was already on stage, covered by paint-spattered dust sheets.

'Act II is set in an apartment in London - pre-set behind Act I, an angled ceiling flat and back wall about halfway upstage. When this was flown out it revealed Act III – a penthouse in New York. The final revelation of the real height and depth of the stage always seems to shock audiences – even the regulars. Their short memories allow us to play all sorts of tricks on them.'

Director: Ian Forrest
Designer: Nettie Edwards
Lighting designer: Michael E Hall

THESE IMAGES HAVE BEEN SPONSORED BY EVERYMAN THEATRE, CHELTENHAM

Act I

Act II

Act III

PICKWICK PAPERS

Charles Dickens, adapted by Ellis Jones

Everyman Theatre, Cheltenham, October 1991

Nettie Edwards: 'This production celebrated the theatre's centenary and the design is as much a celebration of Frank Matcham's energetic auditorium as of anything else. The proscenium is higher than it is wide and in trying to solve the problems of sightline, the only solution is often to exploit the height. This set was a box of magic tricks and corny theatricality. The lighting rig was so high that our electricians had to learn to abseil to rig and focus.'

Director: Michael Houghton
Designer: Nettie Edwards
Lighting designer: Michael E Hall

THE JUNGLE BOOK

Rudyard Kipling, adapted by Patrick Sandford

Nuffield Theatre, Southampton, December 1993

Juliet Shillingford: 'The paintings of Rousseau provided a starting point for the design. I particularly liked the strong use of colour: vivid oranges and blues contrasting with dark greens and blacks. I wanted the images to be illustrative rather than realistic, no fake fur or plastic leaves. The adaptation was very close to the Kipling stories so I used Indian influence in the costumes looking at pictures of temple carvings and ritual dance costumes.'

Director: Patrick Sandford
Set designer: Juliet Shillingford
Lighting designer: Stephen Watson
Original music: Neil Brand

WHEN WE ARE MARRIED

J B Priestley

Everyman Theatre, Cheltenham
October 1990

David Cockayne: 'Three couples discover they were not actually married 25 years earlier. The set was a response to this in that it incorporated two conflicting perspective structures. The steeply raked stage floor increased the impact of the performers in the space and projected the stage through the proscenium arch.'

Director: Fine Time Fontayne
Designer: David Cockayne
Lighting designer: Nick Hunt

ASSASSINS

Book by John Weidman
Music and lyrics by Stephen Sondheim

Library Theatre, Manchester
October 1993

Judith Croft: 'The Library Theatre has a small stage with little wing space and no flying facilities, but it is a wonderfully intimate theatre with a great relationship between audience and performance. Designing for a musical of such complexity in so limited a space brought me to design a shiny black box of tricks, with trucks that slid away to be redressed, a trap door, flags dropping from above and a back-projection screen serviced by five projectors and more than 120 slides. My intention was to provide rapidly changing visual images which complemented the vast range of this exciting musical.'

Director: Roger Haines
Designer: Judith Croft
Lighting designer: Nick Richings
Choreographer: David Needham
Photo credit: Phil Cutts

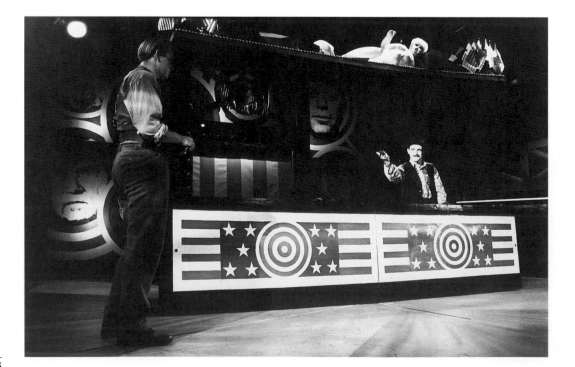

LA BETE

David Hirson

Shoctor Stage at Citadel Theatre, Edmonton, Canada, January 1993

Ann Curtis: 'The play, though taking place in 1654, uses language and syntax so unmistakably modern that the production was set in 1994. Our silver and elegantly abstracted set was as much 20th as 17th century and the company of classical actors into which Valère, the vulgar street busker is introduced, was in modern dress.

'The only 17th-century-type clothes were the costumes worn by Valère in his own clown's outfit to perform his Act II playlet and by Dorine, the stage-struck servant who communicates only by histrionic dumb-show, dressed in theatrical finery borrowed from the company's wardrobe.'

Director: Robin Phillips
Set designer: Hisham Ali
Costume designer: Ann Curtis
Lighting designer: Louise Guinand

HEARTBREAK HOUSE

George Bernard Shaw

His Majesty's Theatre, Perth, Western Australia Angel Productions, July 1994

Voytek: 'A wonderfully restored Edwardian theatre: stage 10m wide by 18.2m deep, with a proscenium height of 9.1m. The play called for an interior and an exterior in what Shaw saw as his Chekovian play.

'The play was set in a house built partly as a ship by Captain Shotover, an old sailor and inventor. Basing the set on a ship propelled by sail and steam alike, it was possible to centre it on a funnel (interior) and a mast (exterior). The funnel contained the captain's cabin and a hatch. The atmosphere was provided by impressionistic brushwork lit from behind and fragments of ship wrapped up in a Klimt landscape like minced meat in a cabbage leaf.'

Director: Bernard Wright
Designer: Voytek
Lighting designer: Stephen Wyckham
Photo credit: Stephen Wyckham

THE MASTERBUILDER

Henrik Ibsen

Bristol Old Vic, November 1992

Sally Crabb: 'The set needed to reflect the inner torments of Solness who feels his powers are failing. These feelings ultimately drive him to reject God from the steeple of his newly completed church. He lives in a clinical, loveless, coldly architectural world. The set was a chamber of tilting boxes receding upstage to a vanishing point which suggested both solidity and instability. The odd perspectives and angles helped to metamorphose the environment to allow us to witness from the top of the steeple the final cathartic moment looking down at where the Masterbuilder lies spread-eagled on the ground.'

Director: Paul Unwin
Designer: Sally Crabb
Lighting designer: Rory Dempster

AN IDEAL HUSBAND
Oscar Wilde

Plymouth Theatre Royal, March 1993

Hugh Durrant: 'The very large stage at Plymouth was filled by a huge peacock – a metaphor for Lady Chiltern's view of her husband. Its tail defined and restricted the acting area but without dwarfing the actors. It also acted as a sounding board, deflecting the words into the auditorium. To hold their own on such a large stage, the costume silhouettes of the Countess of Basildon and Mrs Marchmont had to be big and bold, with strong detailing for those audience members sitting close to the stage. No attempt was made at period cutting. The brief was to allude to the 1890s in a modern couturier's style. The clothes were the colour of money. In contrast to the silhouette and style of her London contemporaries, Mrs. Cheveley, who had lived abroad, wore clothes inspired by the works of Klimt.'

Director: Amanda Knott
Designer: Hugh Durrant
Lighting designer: Mark Prichard
Photo credit: Lawrence Watson

SHADOWLANDS
William Nicholson

Belgrade Theatre, Coventry, October 1992

Adrian Rees: 'We wanted to find a visual link between CS Lewis's academic life and the world of Narnia. We found it on a visit to Magdalen College, Oxford, where, stone pillars supporting figures from mythology and antiquity ring the edge of the quadrangle. We substituted figures from the *Chronicles of Narnia* and used the pillars to frame our acting area and span the space between proscenium and auditorium, taking the focus of the intimate scenes as near to the audience as possible. The figures looking down were a constant reminder of the magic in his work.'

Director: Rumu Sen-Gupta
Designer: Adrian Rees
Lighting designer: Tim Wratten
Photo credit : Robert Lapworth

THIS IMAGE HAS BEEN SPONSORED BY THE BELGRADE THEATRE, COVENTRY

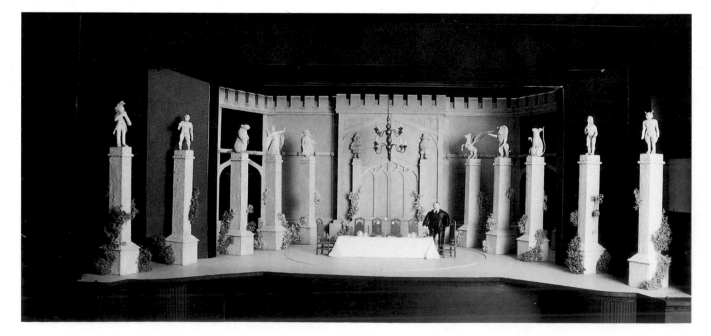

MACBETH

William Shakespeare

Theatre Clwyd, Mold
August 1994

Pamela Howard: 'Actors are scenery. This production uses actors, their groupings and their costumes to create the locations on the saucer-shaped slope that forms the acting space on the stage. When thinking about designing a play, I think first about the staging. I work from the actors outwards, with the aim of presenting the human being in a powerful and dramatic way.

'My second preoccupation is to cast the fabrics the actors wear. If the fabric is wrong for the part, no amount of redesigning will get the right performance out of it. Every time someone asks, "Are you doing Macbeth in period?" I wonder what it means? What period? These people are a mixture of time and culture. Oxfam coats with ancient robes – guns and swords – living by survival.

'Macbeth has himself crowned at Scone and gives a banquet to celebrate, he wears the coronation robe previously worn by the murdered Duncan, but it is too big for him. Lady MacBeth wears a dress made from the royal family plaid. The coronation robe is a patchwork of antique textiles, buttons, jewels, heirlooms of the past history of the clan. It is not a joyful celebration.

'The Witches' kitchen (left): on an empty stage, lit from below, the witches cast their spell. The scene is based on the Isle of Iona, described by the leader of its Christian community as "like a thin piece of tissue paper that separates the material from the spiritual world". The witches are present throughout the play, beneath the floor.'

Director: Helena Kaut-Howson
Designer: Pamela Howard
Lighting designer: Nic Beadle
Choreographer: Kathryn Hunter
Photo credit: Philip Cutts

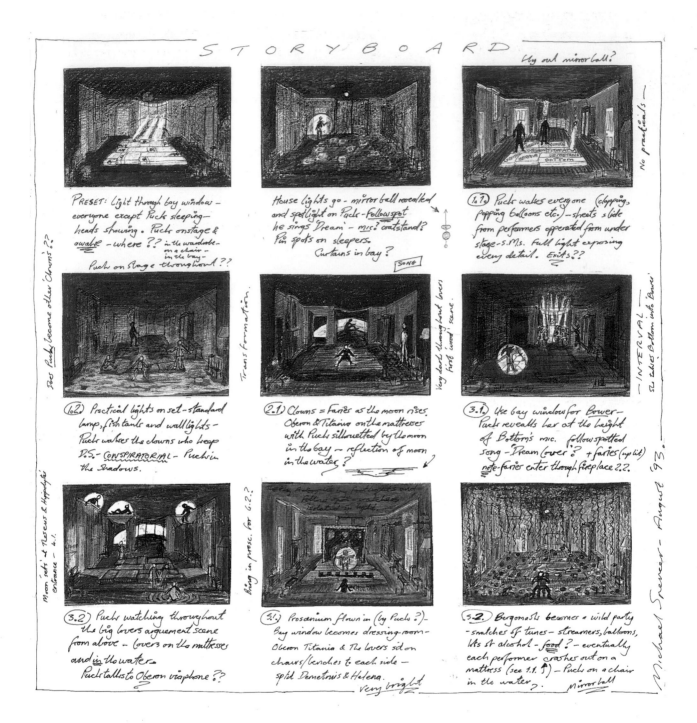

A MIDSUMMER NIGHT'S DREAM

William Shakespeare

Harrogate Theatre, October 1993

Michael Spencer: 'The director, Andrew Manley, and I spent a long time struggling to create a space analogous to the play. Our problem was that as with any *Dream* there were no logical parameters. Eventually we discovered the magic in what was ostensibly a box set, derived from Magritte, which gave us a real scenario in which to place our ideas. It became everyone's dream; an escape from the normality surrounding us. The room was slipping into water, the moon was impossibly large. Puck became the voyeur, the MC... and the party began.'

Director: Andrew Manley
Designer: Michael Spencer
Lighting designer: Jackie Staines

LITTLE SHOP OF HORRORS
Alan Menken and Howard Ashman

Oldham Coliseum Theatre, September 1993

Keith Orton: 'Oldham Coliseum is a proscenium format venue with music hall-style levels and seating arrangements. This means any design for this stage has to be set forward and centrally and its low proscenium makes it difficult to use high levels successfully. With *Little Shop of Horrors*, I played on its B movie and comic book theme. I created a three-dimensional comic book with drawn perspective to create a feeling of depth, but without using the full stage. Also, by setting the shop on an angle, the focus was automatically pushed forward and drawn to the centre of the stage.'

Director: Lindsay Dolan
Designer: Keith Orton
Lighting designer: Shaun Woodhouse

BLITHE SPIRIT
Noel Coward

Britten Theatre, Royal College of Music, London
John Lewis Partnership Dramatic Society
October 1993

Sue Ayers: 'Apart from its strong period flavour, the piece has many practical requirements which are unavoidable for the designer: specific pieces of furniture, French windows and so on. The director also required the presence of spirits other than those in the script who could come and go at will. We achieved this ephemeral atmosphere by having no doors, by incorporating an upper level or other world, by the use of gauze walls and some magical lighting by Paul Hastie.'

Director: Jo Stone
Designer: Sue Ayers
Lighting designer: Paul Hastie

DANCE '90

Center of Theater Arts, Cornell University, USA
March 1990

Chris Watts: 'This dance piece was about four elements – water, earth, wind and sky/air. Lighting was used to project each element through the piece. The four areas on the cyclorama represent the elements, depicting their status over us all.'

Choreographer: Doug Rankin
Lighting designer: Chris Watts

TORQUATO TASSO
Johann Wolfgang Von Goethe

Royal Lyceum Theatre, Edinburgh
August 1994

Hilary Baxter: 'Goethe's 18th-century play about a 16th-century poet was updated to the early 20th century in order to capture the paranoia of an artist within a uniquely privileged society. The costumes (these are for the Footmen) were designed during the rehearsal period to maximise the collaboration with the performers and creative team. The final designs were subtle enough to allow the characters to emerge through their well dressed fashions. Touches of gold were used throughout, as accessories on the men and incorporated into the fragile Klimt-like patterns on the women's dresses.'

Director: Robert David MacDonald
Set designer: Julian McGowan
Costume designer: Hilary Baxter
Lighting designer: Gerry Jenkinson

MACBETH
William Shakespeare

Churchill Theatre, Bromley and tour
National Youth Theatre of Great Britain
April 1994

Brian Lee: 'All the venues were proscenium houses, which fitted with my feeling that the piece should be kept at some distance from the audience, allowing enough scale for battles and the supernatural but enough intimacy for introspective moments.

'Working behind the proscenium was a major bonus in being able to change constantly the stage picture. The black marble changed from wet rock to a sumptuous interior, the steel towers from eerie monoliths to fortress to cage, and the distorted two-way mirrors from land and skyscape to supernatural gateway; an all observing, ever enclosing trap. I collaborated again with Hugh Vanstone on some lighting magic, making these transformations work without laborious scene changes to break the flow.'

Hugh Vanstone: 'In the lighting, I wanted to convey the elemental imagery that powers the play. Brian Lee's stylish design with its clean lines and startling rake largely left the lighting to provide the sense of time and location. In the dagger speech, Macbeth was drawn towards a beam of light in the air, while back-projected, scudding clouds removed him from the present to a 'floating space' of the imagination. Smoke and wind machines were used to provide different atmospheres with deliverate use made of beams of light in the air.'

Director: Edward Wilson
Designer: Brian Lee
Lighting designer: Hugh Vanstone
Photo credit: Stuart Colwill

THESE IMAGES HAVE BEEN SPONSORED BY NATIONAL YOUTH THEATRE OF GREAT BRITAIN

King Charles France II.N

Constable

Henry V

William Shakespeare

**Royal Shakespeare Theatre
Stratford-Upon-Avon,
Royal Shakespeare Company, May 1994**

Kandis Cook: 'The costumes were in period with alterations to stylise the difference between the English and the French. The English were to look like metal dogs, insensitive to the poetry the French were akin to. It was important to fit the shapes and colours of the characters into the emotional world described in the play, and colour itself was a very strong element.'

*Director: Matthew Warchus
Set designer: Neil Warmington
Costume designer: Kandis Cook
Lighting designer: Charles Edwards
Composer: Mark Vibrans*

SUNSET BOULEVARD

Andrew Lloyd Webber, Christopher Hampton and
Don Black, based on the Billy Wilder film

Adelphi Theatre, London
The Really Useful Theatre Company, July 1993

John Napier: 'The challenge lay in recreating for the
stage a film whose sets and set pieces are as legendary
as the script and the performances. There is no
possibility of fulfilling in a theatre anything a film
can do. You can't do a real pan or tracking shot
through corridors and up the stairs into the bedroom;
you can't do real swimming pools and real car chases
because it just looks ludicrous on stage. What you
can do is try to give the essence of the film.

'A lot of the technical complexity has to do with
what's going on offstage rather than on. This is all
the more critical with no music to cover the scene
changes, so the mansion glides into place on a
tracking-lift.

'Some 70% of the show takes place inside Norma's
home which, like the former silent movie queen herself, has seen better days. I studied photographs of
the grand American cinemas of the 1920s and '30s;
a great mish-mash of styles – Gothic, Mexican, Art
Deco, Empire. By contrast, the exterior scenes give a
kind of Los Angeles lightness and airiness suggested
by painters such as David Hockney and Edward
Hopper.'

Director: Trevor Nunn
Set designer: John Napier
Costume designer: Anthony Powell
Lighting designer: Andrew Bridge
Musical staging: Bob Avian
Photo credit: Donald Cooper

ONCE ON THIS ISLAND

Lynn Ahrens and Stephen Flaherty

The Island Theatre (formerly The Royalty Theatre), London

Imagination Entertainments, September 1994

Kendra Ullyart: 'This is a love story, stage managed by the Gods, on an island of the French Antilles inhabited by poor peasant labourers and rich French aristocrats. The design had to combine the savage brutality of the elements with the aura of paradise.

'Essentially this was achieved with a sculptural design where lines, spirals and circles merged and moved through a revolving spiral – a road to nowhere. The never-ending, blue-green sea line contained the space as far as the eye could see, but the acting area was given a more personal setting by including huts with attendant palm trees, and inlets of water bordered by a circular wooden walkway.

'From within the borders another walkway rose above the sea and into the sky to provide the Gods with a route between their heavenly existence and their earthly duties.'

Directors: David Toguri and Gwenda Hughes
Designer: Kendra Ullyart
Lighting designer: Hugh Vanstone
Choreographer: David Toguri
Musical director: Richard Balcombe
Photo credit: Mark Livermore

COPACABANA
Barry Manilow

Prince of Wales Theatre, London
Barry Clayman Concerts, June 1994

Hugh Durrant: 'The White Showgirl costume is part of the all-white opening number of this musical fantasy, representing the blank page on to which the hero will eventually write the song *Copacabana*. Designed primarily for the fairly intimate space of the Prince of Wales Theatre, this musical had an extensive pre-London tour including Plymouth, Manchester and the 3000-seat Edinburgh Playhouse, requiring strong shapes with interesting details.

'Sweet Heaven Showgirl (below right) was originally conceived as a costume for a striptease opening to Act II, the number was subsequently moved to form the resolution to the act, minus the strip! Each girl wears a different sign of the Zodiac, and the jewelled appliqué and mass of feathers help to indicate the opulence of a nightclub show.'

Hugh Vanstone: 'In a departure from my normal ethic, the lighting is highly coloured, fast, flashy and often 'lighting for lighting's sake'. The show as staged in a ludicrously short space of time and the main problem was finding enough time on stage to light it. Working with fully projected scenery I had to work doubly hard on moulding and definition.'

Director: Roger Redfarn
Design concept: Imagination
Set designer: Martin Grant
Costume designer: Hugh Durrant
Lighting designer: Hugh Vanstone
Choreographer: Dorian Sanchez

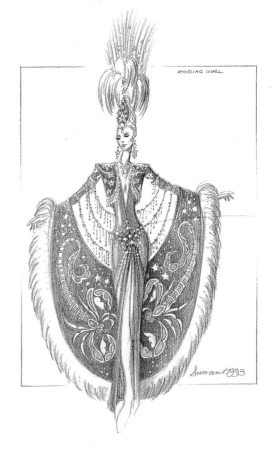

BLOOD BROTHERS
Willy Russell

Theater Heilbronn, Germany
April 1991

David Burrows with TAD:14: 'The set for *Blood Brothers* was designed by a non-hierarchical group of 14 designers, TAD:14. This was an experiment attempting to discover any benefits of designing by committee. Conceptual diversity guaranteed that ideas flowed thick and fast with ever present, objective critical scrutiny. No blocks and few blind alleys. Many hands made light work of the model making and working drawings. The 21-day design period became practical. Deadlines were comfortably met.

'Designing for an excellently equipped modern theatre (built in 1982) challenged us to invent, as unpredictably as possible, a sequence of images which could support the action of this episodic, Liverpudlian musical saga.'

Director: Phil Young
Set designers: TAD:14
Costume and lighting designer: David Burrows
Photo credit: Jürgen Frahm

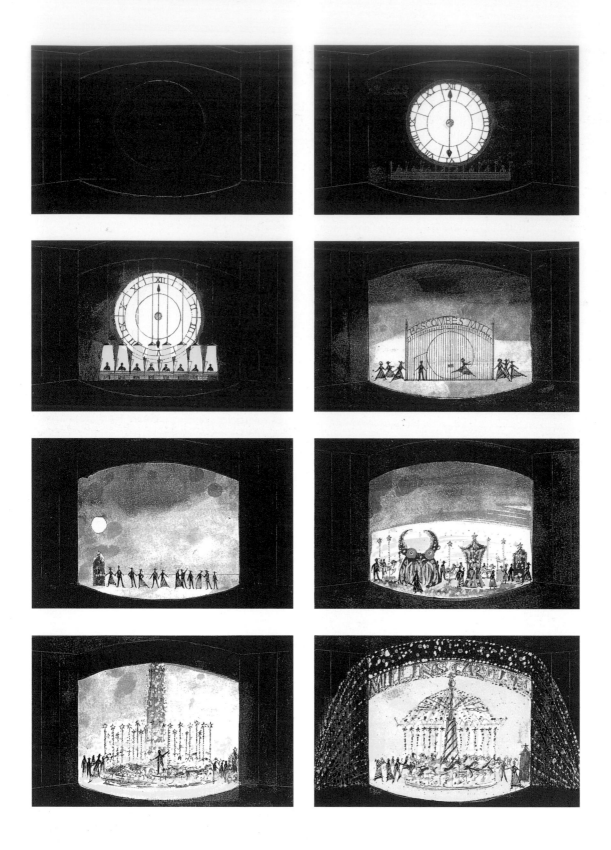

CAROUSEL

Rodgers and Hammerstein

**Lyttleton Theatre, Royal National Theatre
December 1992**

Bob Crowley: 'Early in June 1992 Nick Hytner and I travelled to New England to research our production of Carousel.

Whilst driving up the coast of Maine we came across one of the last remaining Shaker communities in America, Sabbathday Lake. They showed us into their original Meeting House, built in the early 1800s. The walls were painted a beautiful indigo blue to symbolise Heaven. From that small blue New England room where the Shakers used to congregate to pray, sing and dance grew the image of the empty blue box with the revolving floor which is the essence of the design.'

The storyboard represents the opening sequence of the show.

Director: Nicholas Hytner
Choreographer: Kenneth MacMillan
Designer: Bob Crowley
Lighting designer: Paul Pyant

RENARD

Igor Stravinsky

Royal Opera House, Covent Garden
Royal Ballet, February 1994

Bruce McLean: 'The story of *Renard* tells of a narcissistic cock who jealously rules his roost. His domain is policed by a cat and a goat, two rather sinister characters with a penchant for brutality. They are constantly on the lookout for the fox (Renard), whose fitful presence creates an air of nervous tension. Here we see the cock and hens in a celebratory dance, enjoying the freedom of the barnyard again after the fox has finally been killed.

'In conceiving the visual aspect of the ballet, the aim was to suggest a rural landscape with a series of interrelated flat surfaces of bold colour. Although the set suggests a perspective, it creates a two-dimensional look, in keeping with the artificial nature of the original story. The choice of colours helps to strengthen the dark, brooding atmosphere and the feeling of foreboding which are present in both music and text.'

Choreographer: Ashley Page
Designer: Bruce McLean
Lighting designer: Simon Bennison
Photo credit: Bill Cooper

ROMEO AND JULIET

Sergei Prokofiev

Grand Théâtre de Genève
Ballet du Genève, October 1990

Andrew Storer: 'These photographs show three of the principal settings. My initial idea for the set was based on a piazza where all the action would take place. During discussions with the choreographer this was gradually refined into the two houses of Montague and Capulet that stand on either side of the stage throughout the production. Visually these helped to frame the stage in the different theatres and to reinforce the false perspective of the painted floor. Their colour also related to the colour scheme of the costumes of the two families.'

Choreographer: Robert North
Design and lighting: Andrew Storer
Photo credit: Marc Van Appleghem

Daphnis and Chloë

Maurice Ravel

Royal Opera House, Covent Garden
The Royal Ballet, November 1994

Martyn Bainbridge: 'A Greek island, sun, sea, shady olive groves and glorious music; a visual response to Ravel's ballet will be influenced by these inviting impressions. The piece is a three-scene ballet lasting 55 minutes, which was designed for the large stage of the Royal Opera House. The stage space is defined by stone walls on which are incised, in classical Greek, fragments of the original text of *Daphnis and Chloë* by the poet Longus. The shimmering heat of the south is evoked by numerous horizontal strands which are stretched across the stage on four frames.'

Choreographer: Frederick Ashton
Designer: Martyn Bainbridge
Lighting designer: Mark Henderson

GISELLE

Adolphe Adam

Palace Theatre, Manchester and tour
English National Ballet, October 1994

Charles Cusick Smith: 'This was a concentrated effort to avoid adopting the usual open arena for dance with the very familiar legs and borders. Instead I designed a very structured architectural surrounding, set in 1919 just before the Austro-Hungarian Empire was dissolved. The ballet's music is the epitome of a classical romantic ballet. The courtiers are dressed in couture after the designers Paquin and Georges Barbier. The peasants still have a romantic look but without all the ethnic trimmings. There is a large procession of both the courtiers and the villagers from the vineyards to the right or out of the hotel gardens to the left. The large vista of the Austrian Alps in the background is intended to give a broad fresh landscape in complete contrast to the gloomy, covered-in, cavernous dome of branches in Act II.'

Choreographer: Derek Deane
Designer: Charles Cusick Smith
Lighting designer: Paul Pyant
Photo credit: Phil R Daniels

THESE IMAGES HAVE BEEN SPONSORED BY ENGLISH NATIONAL BALLET

THE NUTCRACKER
Peter Illyich Tchaikovsky
Scenario by Marius Petipa

Olympia Theatre, Dublin
Dublin City Ballet, December 1990

Rosemarie Cockayne: 'Designing for ballet after one has been a ballerina is like an extension of movement. One knows how it feels to dance in an area with too many props so it is important to provide sufficient space to dance. In designing *Nutcracker* I wanted it to be a children's colour book coming to life with the charaters emerging from the backcloth to dance.

'In Act I, Dr Drosselmeyer produces dolls for the children – Harlequin and Columbine who, when wound up, do a little dance. Harlequin's costume has brightly coloured diamonds which hint at the cascade of sweets which becomes the theme for Act II, The Kingdom of Sweets, shown above.'

Choreographer: Pearl Gaden
Designer: Rosemarie Cockayne
Lighting designer: Paddy Farrell

PLAYING AWAY

Benedict Mason and Howard Brenton

**The Grand Theatre, Leeds and tour
Opera North and Munich Biennale Festival
May 1994**

*Director: David Pountney
Designers: Huntley Muir
Lighting designer: Paul Pyant
Conductor: Paul Daniel*

GLORIANA

Benjamin Britten

The Grand Theatre, Leeds and tour
Opera North, December 1993

Anthony Ward: 'Gloriana was the incandescent nucleus – the axis – around which Elizabethan England revolved. Britten alternates the public and private scenes. Throughout both, Elizabeth is constantly surveyed by her scheming courtiers and fickle subjects. There were three main elements to the set. A huge gilded box represented the golden Elizabethan Age. Inside this perched public galleries allowing the action within to be spied and commented upon. The Queen is born aloft in her own Sanctum – imprisoned yet free.'

Director: Phyllida Lloyd
Designer: Anthony Ward
Lighting designer: Rick Fisher
Choreographer: Kate Flatt
Photo credit: Donald Cooper

ELEKTRA

Richard Strauss

Dorothy Chandler Pavilion
and the Bastille Opera, Paris
Los Angeles Music Center Opera Association
February 1990

John and Elizabeth Bury: 'Big stages – huge roles! So clarify the concept. Give everybody the dignity and clarity of an image to which they and we can relate. Noble voices – not to be hindered by cluttered space. Real acting and gymnastic challenges, contemporary directorial concepts abound. But this is a classic, nothing must look difficult or contrived – it must just happen!'

Director: David Pountney
Design and lighting: John Bury
Costume designers: John and Elizabeth Bury

HANSEL AND GRETEL

Engelbert Humperdinck

Sydney Opera House
Australian Opera, July 1992

Mark Thompson: 'The first scene is contained within a small naturalistic room. When the children are sent into the forest their world explodes into a nightmare of fears and phobias. All the elements are rooted in the first set – even the kitchen clock becomes an ominously hostile moon. '

Director: Elijah Moshinsky
Designer: Mark Thompson
Lighting designer: Nigel Levings
Photo credit: Branco Gaica

TURANDOT

Giacomo Puccini

Ashcroft Theatre, Croydon
Surrey Opera, June 1994

Perspective Three: 'Turandot pleads with her father not to honour the agreement after Calaf has answered all three riddles to win her hand in marriage.'

Director: Christopher Cowell
Set designer: Tessa Scott
Costume designer: Amanda Benwell
Lighting designer: Jon Driscoll
Photo credit: Robert Muller

DER ROSENKAVALIER

Richard Strauss and Hugo Von Hofmannsthal

London Coliseum

English National Opera, February 1994

Peter J Davison: 'The aim of the set was to create three related spaces using the minimum materialistic detail. Act I created a sophisticated and effortlessly elegant environment for the Marschallin in contrast to the ostentatious bourgeois and parvenu world of Faninal in the second. The configuration of the space remained the same for all Acts, expanding in the second to allow a corridor of glass and light which could contain the household and provide Octavian with a processional entrance for the presentation of the Rose.'

Director: Jonathan Miller
Set designer: Peter J Davison
Costume designer: Sue Blane
Lighting designer: Jean Kalman

THE JEWEL BOX

Wolfgang Amadeus Mozart/Griffiths

Grand Theatre, Leeds and tour
Opera North, February 1991

Anthony Baker: 'The image above shows the world of the composer downstage, with a harpsichord falling into the pit and a coat, wig and cane resting on the proscenium. Beyond the white floor and railing is a deep blue velvet curtain, a panel of which has swagged to reveal a tiny stage set for an 18th-century comic opera.

'The image to the right shows the basic set for *The Jewel Box*. A panel in the soft cyclorama has just lifted to allow the composer's father to enter the space.'

Director: Francisco Negrin
Designer: Anthony Baker
Lighting designer: David Cunningham
Photo credit: Richard H Smith

THE CUNNING LITTLE VIXEN
Leos Janacek

Royal Opera House, London
The Royal Opera, June 1990

Director: Bill Bryden
Designer: William Dudley
Lighting designer: Robert Bryan
Choreographer: Stuart Hopps
Conductor: Simon Rattle
Photo credit: Clive Barda

GAWAIN
Harrison Birtwistle

Royal Opera House, London
The Royal Opera, May 1991

Director: Di Trevis
Designer: Alison Chitty
Lighting designer: Paul Pyant
Movement director: Jane Gibson
Conductor: Elgar Howarth
Photo credit: Clive Barda

WERTHER
Massenet

Sir Jack Lyons Theatre, London
Royal Academy of Music, February 1994

Richard Aylwin: 'Massenet wrote *Werther* in 1892. For this production we created a shifting emotional space; a double exposure of nature and a silvery reflection of Goethe's stories. The space (which was a simple development of the proscenium) closed in layers of changing realities, feelings and predictions. Every image, based closely on the pastels of Redon, was dominated by constantly altering emotional colour.'

Director: Ceri Sherlock
Set designer: Richard Aylwin
Lighting designer: Simon Calder
Photo credit: Eleni Leoussi

FAUST
Charles Gounod

Ashcroft Theatre, Croydon
Surrey Opera, June 1993

Julian Adams: 'With a theatre where the audience looks up at the stage instead of on to it, the top two thirds of the performance space become quite important. The suspended star seemed to be the perfect solution as it came to symbolise Mephistopheles' influence on the opera. By placing it on the house winches it could lift and tilt, allowing further scenery to fly in and around it. In the last Act, the star came down to imprison Marguerite where, for the final aria, it was unhooked at the back and flown out completely.'

Director: Christopher Cowell
Designer: Julian Adams
Lighting designer: Chris Davey

THE LOVE OF THREE ORANGES

Sergei Prokofiev

**Det Kongelige Teaters, Copenhagen
The Royal Opera, October 1994**

Joe Vanek: 'Prokofiev's exuberant and surreal fairy tale is open to limitless interpretations. The choreographer, Flemming Flindt, gave a very clear brief. The opera was to inhabit a simplistic, colourful and child-like world that in a post-modern context would echo the criteria of the Ballet Russe designers. Yet there was to be no overt Russian flavour. Post-modern architecture seemed the key to the design, with its strong emphasis on colour and angles, and by mixing Islamic, Tibetan and Moroccan styles in both architecture and costume this hard-edged fantastical world emerged.'

Director: Flemming Flindt
Designer: Joe Vanek

Act I, scene 2, Mother Goose's Brothel

Act II, scene 3, Tom's house

THE RAKE'S PROGRESS

Igor Stravinsky

Lyric Opera Chicago, October 1994

Richard Hudson: 'The set is based on the 18th-century convention of wings and borders, and the scene changes happen in front of the audience as at Drottningholm in Sweden. The sharp acid colours were chosen to make the changes as striking as possible.'

Director: Graham Vick
Designer: Richard Hudson
Lighting designer: Duane Schuler
Photo credit: Robert Workman

Act II, scene 2, The Street

Act II, scene 3, Baba's Posessions

THE KING COMM

Fabienne Audeoud

The Britten Theatre, Royal College of Music, London

The Baylis Programme's New Visions, New Voices, May 1993

Helena Roden: 'This project presented the challenge of how to design and present as a whole event, four completely different operas. Settings ranged from a bedroom, a traffic-jam, a technological space, to the Arctic; and musical styles between Kate Bush and Benjamin Britten. I wanted each opera's individuality to shine through but without making the audience suffer visual indigestion or endless scene changes. My solution was to keep all four pieces very open and uncluttered, and to utilise the flytower to its limit. A white cyclorama and a suspended silver frame were consistent factors in all four operas. Each piece had a distinct but limited theme colour and texture and a minimum of carefully chosen, significant objects.'

Director: Stephen Langridge
Set designer: Helena Roden
Lighting designer: Tom Mannings
Conductor: Peter Selwyn
Photo credit: Sue Adler

WOZZECK

Alban Berg

The Grand Theatre, Leeds and tour
Opera North, May 1993

Hildegard Bechtler: 'Wozzeck looks for the knife with which he killed Marie. The moon, large, round and female bears witness. We don't return to the previous world of hard-edged flats which had, until now, cut the action filmically. Wozzeck prepares for his death and we prepare for the empty white space where we find the child alone.'

Director: Deborah Warner
Set designer: Hildegard Bechtler
Costume designer: Nicky Gillibrand
Lighting designer: Jean Kalman

*Self-contained, quickly and efficiently
assembled, light but robustly constructed,
these are the criteria by which a touring set
is assessed. It must boldly occupy designated
spaces, no matter how varied, mask in or out
the required widths and heights of the vastly
different theatres used for middle-scale and
number-one tours, and always give the
performers their habitual points of reference.
Theatre-in-education, small-scale and
community tours face a similar challenge but
often without the stage, masking and lighting
and sometimes even without a theatre. In
non-theatre spaces costumes need to
concentrate attention on the performance
and both costumes and elements of set take
on a sculptural significance.*

STREET OF CROCODILES

Adapted by Simon McBurney with Mark Wheatley from stories by Bruno Schultz

Cottesloe Theatre and world tour
Theatre de Complicité and Royal National Theatre
August 1993

Rae Smith: 'The design was created in rehearsal. After four weeks watching and drawing came a week focusing the visual language, and then taking technical matters back to the rehearsal room. This gave the director and actors time to become accustomed to each other and to the props, costumes and set.

'Scenery was an encumbrance so we played the Cottesloe as an empty shell and added the elements which would give a visual fixed point to the ever mutating situations in rehearsals: a stove for the kitchen, the desk units to make the classroom, dining tables, shop counter and so on. The design had to exist seamlessy within the production.

'For touring the set was broken up into units in such a way that each venue would be more an environment than a set: the floor, to determine the playing space; the wall – played against the theatre wall when possible, or a built wall if affordable, or a very basic climbing frame; traps in the floor were used wherever possible, otherwise the doors or the tops of the little sheds were used.

'Coats, books, pots and pans and an excellent scene painter were essential in pulling the environment of the theatre or site into the playing space.'

Director: Simon McBurney
Designer: Rae Smith
Lighting designer: Paule Constable
Choreographer: Christopher Shutt

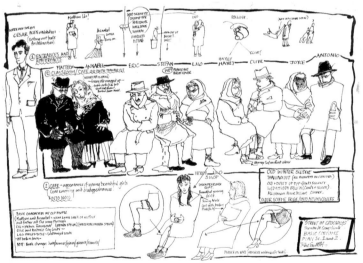

HENRY VI
(THE BATTLE FOR THE THRONE)
William Shakespeare

The Other Place and RSC regional tour
Royal Shakespeare Company, July 1994

Rae Smith: 'The design brief was for a set which would fit into the RSC's touring module and into The Other Place, in Stratford upon Avon.

'Rather than embark on the conceptual world of the History play, I decided to use the sensory world of memory – a poetic reconstruction of the past where the texture of the world would fill the audience with memories and poetic associations: the heavy wooden floor and wall, dank and cold; the damp smell of the forest floor or single blasted pine tree; a church bell; running water; a rusted metal door which shut like a vault; nature at work – armour rusting.'

Director: Katie Mitchell
Designer: Rae Smith
Lighting designer: Tina MacHugh
Choreographer: Paul Allain
Music: Helen Chadwick
Photo credit: Henrietta Butler

ROSES HAVE THORNS
Glasshouses

Leicester Phoenix and tour
Glasshouses, February 1990

Nigel Prabhavalkar: 'This was a new dance piece that toured to a number of different venues. I therefore designed a frame against which to see the performances. This set a scale and mood for the piece. Elements of the choreography were evolved in workshops using the set, props and layers of costume, so that the design became an integral part of the performance.'

Choreographers: Jayne Stevens & Jo Breslin
Designer: Nigel Prabhavalkar
Lighting designer: Simon Gray

AS YOU LIKE IT
William Shakespeare

Cheek by Jowl
July 1991 - April 1992, revived September 1994

Nick Ormerod: '*As You Like It* was played by an all-male cast. Like all Cheek by Jowl's work it also attempted to make a virtue of touring, by using the simplest means to achieve the richest effects. Much emphasis was placed on costume, lighting and colour to make the change from a cold austere court to a forest in winter, to the forest bursting into spring. All of the design decisions were made in the rehearsal period.'

Director: Declan Donnellan
Designer: Nick Ormerod

THE THREE LIVES OF LUCIE CABROL
John Berger, adapted by Simon McBurney and Mark Wheatley, devised by the Company

Riverside Studios and international tour
Theatre de Complicité, January 1994

Tim Hatley: 'I arrived at the designs for Lucie Cabrol by working with the company in rehearsal, and delaying design decisions until the last moment. This resulted in a more thorough understanding of the manipulation of space through design.'

Director: Simon McBurney
Designer: Tim Hatley
Lighting designer: Paule Constable
Sound designer: Catherine Reiser
Photo credit: Wilfred Nicholson

ROUGHCUT

Steve Reich

International tour
Rambert Dance Company, 1991

Tim Hatley: 'A thicket of perspex rods provided the space with simplicity and flexibility, echoing the choreography. The rods moved in and out of the space vertically, at varying speeds either individually or together to create a false ceiling.'

Choreographer: Richard Alston
Designer: Tim Hatley
Lighting designer: Peter Mumford
Photo credit: Catherine Ashmore

THE MAGIC SHOES

Nona Shepphard

National tour

Theatre Centre, December 1993

Marsha Roddy: '*The Magic Shoes* was a dance play in which flow and rhythm were vital. It toured from huge stages to small studio spaces, so it had to be infinitely flexible as two worlds continuously alternated.'

Director: Nona Shepphard
Designer: Marsha Roddy
Lighting designer: Chris White
Choreographer: Jeanefer Jean Charles
Composer: Andy Dodge

THESE IMAGES HAVE BEEN SPONSORED BY THE THEATRE CENTRE

NATURAL FORCES

Devised by the company

Schools tour

Humberside Theatre in Education, May 1994

Louise Ann Wilson: 'The set/installation is a metaphor for conflict between human culture and the natural world. Glass-fronted cabinets containing objects preserved and decaying, growing and transforming, are stacked high. A still-life woman cocooned within a decaying paper dress emerges from her picture frame, ripping her way to the light. A man and a woman trapped within dreams, become disconnected from the world, themselves and each other.'

Director: John Haslett
Designer: Louise Ann Wilson

ROSIE AND JIM'S BIG THEATRE ADVENTURE

Nona Shepphard

National tour

Ragdoll Theatre Productions, September 1993

Marsha Roddy: 'The initial setting is an empty black box. We created three environments: the Dance Set, the Workshop and the Wardrobe, where Rosie and Jim create mayhem. The idea was to introduce a very young audience to the workings of the theatre.'

Director: Nona Shepphard
Designer: Marsha Roddy
Lighting designer: Tim Boyd

THIS IMAGE HAS BEEN SPONSORED BY RAGDOLL THEATRE PRODUCTIONS

EDIBLE CITY

Jayne Newton Chance and Tim Fleming

Tour

West Yorkshire Playhouse Theatre in Schools
May 1994

Madeleine Millar: 'It is rare to work on a piece of theatre-in-education that calls for fantastical costumes. Three spirits tell the story of Promise, a young boy, and the Jewel Bird. I wanted the spirits costumes to have the feeling of rotting flesh, revealing bits of muscle structure beneath. The other characters were presented by the spirits using body masks; Promise was a small face held on the back of the actor's hand.'

Director: Gail McIntyre
Designer: Madeleine Millar
Photo credit: Joan Russell/Guzelian

DESPERATE JOURNEY

Based on Kathleen Fidler's novel

Tour

TAG Theatre Company, April 1994

Kate Borthwick: 'My priority was to create four distinct worlds: a visual difference between the soft, weathered homeland of Scotland and the brave new world of Canada.

'Old stones, a peat fire and woollen clothes were used to represent the colours, feelings and textures of the Celtic homeland.

'The utilitarian, Dickensian way of life in the Glasgow tenements was suggested by geometric panels. Dark, stark colours were used to create the polluted, sad streets and cramped conditions of suffering city people.

'The white sails of the ship embraced the hope and freedom of the emigrants, but could not alleviate the chronic conditions and disease at this stage of their desperate journey.

'Canada demanded a new approach to life. Dynamic angles echoed the shape of the mountains. Strong primary colours and stretched synthetic fibres suggested the survival strategies used in this barren but savage landscape. Snow shoes demanded a new movement in the choreography.'

Director & choreographer: Andrew Howitt
Designer: Kate Borthwick
Lighting design: the company

Borderline Theatre, Ayr

Bowmore Hall, Islay

Kirkwall Arts Theatre, Orkney

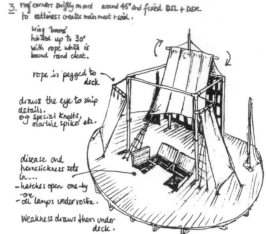

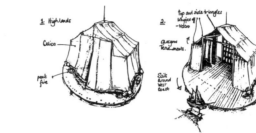

ROMEO AND JULIET

William Shakespeare

Small-scale tour

Theatr Powys, November 1993

Christine Marfleet: 'Brecon Guildhall has a tiny stage, a height of 3.6 m, a low proscenium arch, a raked auditorium, a gallery and spiral staircase get-in. This imposing wall – Verona, savaged by generations of feuding inhabitants – became a crumbling backdrop to a young love story. The tomb was created by the narrow vertical divide which opened in blackout to cast a shaft of backlight across the floor. At Brecon, miraculously, tragedy did not become farce. The wall was reduced in width, Romeo and Juliet crawled on and off the balcony in blackouts; here passion enabled them to lie down, so most of the audience could see!'

Director: Janine Wunsche
Designer: Christine Marfleet
Lighting designer: Paul Howey
Fight director: Steve Wilsher

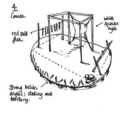

FINDERS KEEPERS

devised by Anthony Burbage, Steve Leyton,
Jan Sharkey-Dodds and Ian Teague

Schools tour
**Greenwich and Lewisham Young People's
Theatre, January 1994**

Ian Teague: '*Finders Keepers* was a full-day,
participatory TIE programme for 9 - 11 year-olds
about the discovery of Roman ruins on the site of a
large property development. During the devising
process, the design became an integral element of
the programme. As a consequence of scenes taking
place in different rooms the young people had
constantly to re-define their relationship with both
the space and the performers.

'Working from a gridded floorcloth and
coordinates, the young people constructed a full-
scale model of a ruined Roman villa, with pieces of
mosaic floor and sections of internal wall. This
created the space for the rest of the day's activities
and became an investment by the participants in that
space.'

Director: Jan Sharkey-Dodds
Designer: Ian Teague

JOURNEY

Devised

Schools tour
Theatr Iollo, May 1992

Polly Richards: '*Journey* was a devised show for
infants, based on the paintings and sculpture of
Picasso, about a captain, a seagull and a painter who
go off to sea. The design was to play a key role in
this production, and the director was keen to reinter-
pret the works through movement, and sounds. In
rehearsal I produced a variety of Picasso-esque
objects, makeshift environments and masks. We
were drawn to his collages and use of found objects,
identifying this creativity with children's play.'

Director: Kevin Lewis
Designer: Polly Richards

TARTUFFE

Molière

Tour
Tara Arts and Royal National Theatre, 1990

Magdalen Rubalcava: 'The basic element of the set
is a tent-like structure; the result of practical,
dramatic and aesthetic considerations. A tent is
light, strong and, when folded, takes up very little
space. It is ideal for a small-scale and international
tour. The tent is also a common structure in Mughal
paintings which I used for reference and which also
inspired my use of colour. The fabric itself was
tennis netting, reflecting an appropriate, old-
fashioned playfulness.'

Director: Jatinder Verma
Designer: Magdalen Rubalcava
Lighting designer: Brien Knox
Photo credit: Brien Knox

ROOMS

Devised

Leicester Haymarket Studio & national tour
Glasshouses Dance Company, November 1993

Nettie Scriven: 'Within the small, darkened space,
Within a space much like a corner,
The small, compact architecture
Repeats itself in three.
No masking.
Just a green and yellow sculpture alone
Animated by silent forms,
Movements of white and red and black.
A glimpse of Hopper.
Within this space,
At the corners of each room,
A woman sits alone
Waiting and Listening.
With the darkness of the night
They enter each other,
They enter each other's space,
Repeating and Multiplying
Playing and Threatening
Crawling the walls
Like spattered bodies on the sidewalk
Seen from a great height.
Frenzied women
Beating the walls down
Going ever deeper and deeper in
as in Bluebeard's chamber,
Needing to reach the smaller, inner door
Before breath. '

Director: Steve Shill
Choreographer: Jo Breslin
Designer: Nettie Scriven
Lighting designer: Christopher Charles
Composer: Michael Burdett
Photo credit: Nicola Tarr

THESE IMAGES HAVE BEEN SPONSORED BY NOTTINGHAM
TRENT UNIVERSITY

THE DAY AFTER TOMORROW

Roel Adam, translated by Noel Clark

Cottesloe Theatre and tour
Royal National Theatre, January 1993

Kate Burnett: '*The Day After Tomorrow* was designed
to play end-on in repertory in the Cottesloe, sitting in
front of sets for the evening shows. It was revived for
a ten-week tour, so it had to be compact and
assembled or dismantled in an hour.

'Two sisters live in an armchair and quarrel a lot.
They go on a journey to find their little brother.
Although not yet born, he has appeared to them in
the night, wrapped in the land of music. After an
encounter with a very odd witch and a fairy they
reach him and help him struggle free before
returning home. We never know whether the sisters
really live in the chair and go on a journey or
whether it is all "pretend". The chair needed to be
familiar, relatively realistic but also strange and
exciting. Because of its size and the possibilities for
adventures, it had to be old, cosy and shabby, to be
home but ,with the covers removed, also a forest, a
mountain and the land of the unborn.'

Director: Anthony Clark
Designer: Kate Burnett
Lighting designer: Ian Fergus
Choreographer: Jane Gibson
Composer: Mark Vibrans

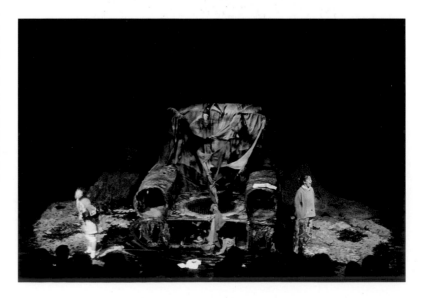

THE LIGHTHOUSE
Peter Maxwell Davies

Tour

Music Theatre Wales, May 1993

Simon Banham: 'This production was first performed on a 6m-diameter platform, suspended 15m up in the air. The range of touring venues demanded a self-contained set that, whilst allowing for its environ-ment, created its own particular atmosphere within each space.'

Director: Michael McCarthy
Designer: Simon Banham
Lighting designer: Ace McCarron
Photo credit: Sheila Burnett

THE GRAPES OF WRATH
John Steinbeck, adapted by Frank Galati

Dundee Repertory Theatre and tour
7:84 Theatre Company and Dundee Repertory Company, February 1994

"The wooden plank set has simple beauty and splashes of theatrical joy, with a real fire, rain and long-johned lads throwing themselves into troughs of water".   THE TIMES

"This design succeeds in evoking the land of America, its farms and farm buildings".
                                    SCOTLAND ON SUNDAY

"This wide screen theatre, emphasised by Mark Leese's simple but dramatic set".   THE HERALD

Director: Iain Reerie
Designer: Mark Leese
Lighting designer: Ian Scott
Musical director: Jon Beales
Photo credit: Sean Hudson

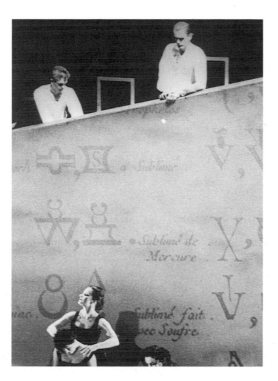

LIVES OF THE GREAT POISONERS
Caryl Churchill

Tour
Second Stride, 1990

Composer: Orlando Gough
Choreographer/co-director: Ian Spink
Co-director: James MacDonald
Designer: Antony McDonald
Lighting designer: Peter Mumford
Photo credits: Rosy Sanders and Robin Morris

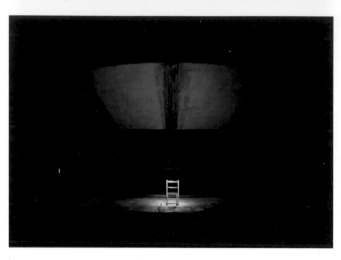
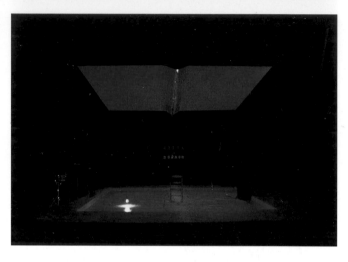

POISONED SILENCE

Devised

Opera North Community and Education tour, June 1993

Ian Sommerville: 'Poisoned Silence was devised and written by students at Dewsbury College in conjunction with Opera North's production of Wozzeck. It was performed in parallel with the main company in small venues and was the company's first design-led project. The design evolved first in response to a domestic killing reported in a local newspaper. The opera was written afterwards around the design. The design had to represent a slow process of decay and a breakdown of human relationships. I wanted to create a neutral space like a blank canvas the mood and location of which could be changed by the use of light.'

Director: Stephen Langridge
Design and lighting: Ian Sommerville

L'ELISIR D'AMORE ▶

Donizetti

Touring
English Touring Opera
October 1993

Isabella Bywater: 'I have worked with Stephen Medcalf several times and we had a very similar response to the piece. We recognised that it was charming and naïve but that we should avoid sentiment. I had to listen to it a few times before I could get rid of depressing, cute, folkloric images of operatic 1880s peasants. We decided that if it was transplanted to mid-west America in the 1930s we could probably retain the naivety of the plot, the innocence of the characters and the truth of the emotions but avoid too much sweetness.

'The quality of heat and hard work and the desire for shade on a hot day were important too. I looked at pictures by Balthus, Van Gogh and Hugh Dunford Wood for inspiration, and decided on just yellow and blue, for light and shade to represent a convincing heat, even in an English autumn.'

Producer: Stephen Medcalf
Designer: Isabella Bywater
Lighting Designer: Kevin Sleep

IDOMENEO
Wolfgang Amadeus Mozart
Tour
Welsh National Opera, September 1991

Costumes for Arbace, Elettra, Idamante, Court of Neptune.
Director: Howard Davies
Set designer: William Dudley
Costume designer: Liz da Costa
Lighting designer: Alan Burrett
Choreographer: Stuart Hopps

DANCING LEDGE

Coliseum Theatre, London
English National Ballet, July 1990

David Buckland: 'Dancing Ledge opened to a stage occupied by 6.5m-high figures hanging in space, around which dancers performed. The figures were set in motion and contained small pieces of photographic information which made them particular, almost portraits. These then departed to reveal a 13.5m x 2m drum revolving slowly in space above the dancers' heads, suspended without any visible lines.The drum was gold-plated and its surface was punctured with cut-out shapes echoing ancient seas. Inside it were some 40 lanterns which traced the ancient sea shapes across the floor, the red backdrop, the ceiling and the audience as the drum revolved. The speed varied and it could rotate at up to 30 rpm. It was the vision of and from a body passing through space above the surface of the world.'

Choreographer: Siobhan Davies
Designer: David Buckland
Lighting designer: Peter Mumford

OS MISTERIOS DE CHESTER
Anon

Teatro Circo, Braga, Portugal
London Theatre Ensemble, March 1992

Claudia Mayer: 'The set was largely designed before we arrived in Portugal for the rehearsals, but I felt we needed to allow for the influence of the location, and the development of the piece itself. The space developed throughout the play, from an emptiness at the start of the Old Testament to an urban New Testament of walls, (interior and exterior).'

Director: Mark Dornford-May
Designer: Claudia Mayer
Lighting designer: Ace McCarron
Photo credit: Jorge Figueras

DIFFERENT TRAINS

Steve Reich

Sadlers Wells Theatre and international tour
Siobhan Davies Dance Company

David Buckland: 'The music, played live, describes the passage of train journeys across the USA in 1941-42 and those of Jews simultaneously being sent to concentration camps in Germany. The text sounds are recordings. The set is of steel construction and fresnel lenses, inspired by New York's Grand Central Station. In front, two blades, one 6m in diameter, rotate at different speeds and contain images of maps, trains and Duchamp-like marks. There are periods of total calm on the stage; at others the dancers perform on staircases of light.'

Choreographer: Siobhan Davies
Designer: David Buckland

LES ENFANTS DU PARADIS

Jacques Prevert adapted by Mike Alfreds

Tour
Cambridge Theatre Company and David Glass Ensemble, September 1993

Designer Paul Dart: 'The trussing was used to create a theatre within the stage space - which then had another smaller stage space within that. All the flying, swings and drop cloths, were operated from within the trussing framework. This enabled myself and the crew to create a very complex show that could tour easily. To make the trussing look old it was lagged with fabric.'

Directors: Mike Alfreds and David Glass
Design and lighting: Paul Dart
Photo credit: Simon Annand

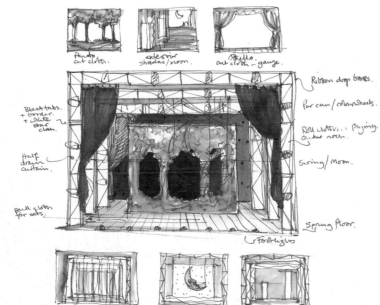

TIMETRAX

Devised by the company
Music by James Mackie

Small-scale tour
Ludus Dance Company, January 1993

Ashley Shairp: 'This show was about a train-spotter falling on the rail tracks and being swept into a time tunnel. After various encounters he came across four 18th-century Court Ladies. The sequence mixed courtly dance with Madonna's vogue and ended in revolution, with wigs and frocks being ripped off and the Ladies dancing horizontally across the floor with make-up smeared faces. The wigs were the main challenge, having to be incredibly light and secure and yet easily removable. I borrowed the idea of using swimming caps as bases, and it worked.'

Director: James Mackie
Choreographer: T C Howard
Designer: Ashley Shairp
Lighting designers: Roger Nicholson and James Mackie

A ROOM WITH A VIEW

EM Forster

Yvonne Arnaud Theatre, Guildford and tour
Snap People's Theatre Trust, April 1991

Sarah Ashpole: 'The reversible set was divided into Act I – Italy, and Act II – England, seen through the eyes of the pivotal character, Lucy Honeychurch. Italy was bright and definite but also distorted and slightly sinister, full of hidden dangers and excitement, while England was cool, faded and seemingly more conventional. This production toured to a number of theatre spaces with very different dimensions, therefore it also had to be flexible in practical terms.'

Director: Andy Graham
Set designer: Sarah Ashpole
Costume designer: Gillian Holman
Lighting designer: Paul Franklyn

SELF CATERING, A SHORT HISTORY OF THE WORLD

Andrew Cullen

Tour

Altered States, September 1992

Hannah Mayall: 'This was an existential comedy about five people (Henry Fonda, Clint Eastwood, Marilyn Monroe, Bette Davis and Meryl Streep) marooned on the beach of a desert island. It was a condensed version of human history set in an enclosed location which was representative of the wider world. Non-naturalism was appropriate for the absurdist style of the script. The environment needed to be inhospitable; stones were included to give the actors a physical challenge. The unvarying blue was inspired by the blue superimposition screens used in film studios, and by sea and sky.'

Director: Kate Rowland
Designer: Hannah Mayall
Lighting designer: Jo Town

CONVERTED SPACES

'Half ruined buildings once again take on
The look of buildings waiting to be finished
Generously planned; their fine proportions
Can already be guessed at, but they still
Need our understanding.'

Bertolt Brecht

A space with a past of a different kind
contributes something of itself to the the
theatrical event. idiosyncratic aspects of old
buildings, such as the beams of the
Warehouse Theatre in Croydon, the
shuttered windows in the Almeida's curved
brick wall and the Manchester Dancehouse's
Art Deco gilt work, are scenic elements in
themselves. In reclaiming these spaces, we
make the mark of our own time, by
importing modern materials, installing a
utilitarian metal staircase, dividing a space
with glass or adopting arrangements of
flexible seating, all of which emphasise our
temporary occupancy.

THE TURN OF THE SCREW

Benjamin Britten

Tramway, Glasgow
Scottish Opera, February 1994

Vicki Mortimer: 'Without being too disingenuous, we wanted the design elements to make a "possible" reality in the Tramway; more that light, cutting through the unlit space, would make the "event". The detail of the Tramway's own memories and textures make it difficult to design for, without the space spitting it out as artificial. We decided on very simple elements: tarpaulin, water, ironwork, an earth and bark floor; a large window leaning against one of Peter Brook's walls as if abandoned half way out of the building. Constructing on a site without right angles resulted in a Heath Robinson feel, which was unusual for a Scottish Opera production. All concerned were amazingly tolerant.'

Director: David Leveaux
Designer: Vicki Mortimer
Lighting designer: Alan Burrett
Photo credit: Bill Cooper

BETRAYAL

Harold Pinter

The Almeida Theatre, London

Rick Fisher: 'A woman and her husband's best friend escape from a party and consider an affair. The husband comes in. There is just light from the off-stage world. Catching the characters is a shaft of light which allows them privacy, shadow and highlight, to flirt and question. The director, designer and performers were all involved in making this extreme image work for the scene.'

Director: David Levaux
Designer: Mark Thompson
Lighting designer: Rick Fisher
Photo credit: Ivan Kyncl

OEDIPUS REX

Arnold Schoenberg

The Dancehouse, Manchester
Hallé Orchestra and the Royal Exchange Theatre
July 1994

Vince Herbert: 'The singers were to move through and around the orchestra. The piece was set at the junction of three roads. Runways dissected the orchestra and there was a plinth for the statue-like Oedipus. My brief was to light the performers to look as if they were wearing white masks. They were permitted just one gesture each. The character of the lighting meant that the movement of a white-sleeved arm could illuminate the entire auditorium.'

Director: James McDonald
Set designer: David Roger
Lighting designer: Vince Herbert
Photo credit: Stephen Vaughan

I Ought to be in Pictures

Neil Simon

The Mill at Sonning
June 1994

Bruce Gallup: 'The intention was to take a step away from the naturalistic sets often presented at the Mill and to indicate something of the contrast between Libby's glamorised vision of Hollywood and her father's drab reality. Her strong influence upon his life was shown in Act II by the introduction of colour across the set in the form of painted furniture, rugs, posters and contemporary sculptures.'

Director: Graham Callum
Set designer: Bruce Gallup
Costume designer: Jane Granger
Lighting designer: Roz Nash
Photo credit: Norman Weston

Turner's Crossing

Sheila Dewey

Warehouse Theatre, Croydon
May 1992

Michael Pavelka: 'A marriage of domestic interior and traffic island, gelled by a marshland of yellow clay. The opposition of these worlds has itself been challenged by opposing banks of seats...all bound by the impending fall of the characters' landscapes.'

Director: Ted Craig
Designer: Michael Pavelka
Lighting designer: Douglas Kuhrt
Music: Simon Slater
Photo credit: Paul Thompson

RETREAT FROM MOSCOW

Don Taylor

New End Theatre, London
First Writes, January 1993

David Cockayne: 'A realistic play set in a minimal, part-expressionist space. The interlocking square and circle refer back to the Russian arts of the 1920s and relate to the relationships within the play. The contents of the Lenin poster spill out of their frame and advance across the rear wall of the stage; the colours of the production also related to this poster.'

Director: Don Taylor
Designer: David Cockayne
Lighting designer: Michael E Hall

PICTURE ME

Alex Summers

Attic Theatre, Wimbledon

Christopher Richardson: 'The very quirkiness of the Attic Theatre in Wimbledon provokes imaginative uses. *Picture Me* follows the intrusion of a brilliant but chaotic personality into the life and domain of another, hitherto ordered and tranquil. It mixes present and flash-back, moving from hospital to graveyard and to apartment which to one character is an enfolding security and to the other a frightening maze.

'Steeldecks were the means to imply an upper storey and to make sure everyone could see and Roger Frith's lighting helped to give a moment's reality to the symbolic shapes.'

Director: Richard Osborne
Designer: Christopher Richardson
Lighting designer: Roger Frith

WAY PAST COOL

B'Iye Bandele Thomas

The Tabernacle, Notting Hill, London
Royal Court Young People's Theatre Company,
August 1993

Cathy Ryan: 'This was a specially commissioned play by the Nigerian writer B'Iye Bandele by the RCYPT and the Notting Hill Carnival Association. It was a broad and humorous look at the history of the area since the 1950s, using carnival headresses, masks and a promenade staging. The space is a huge, round, disused church. We erected walkways over the pews and the audience followed the action around the building.'

Director: Burt Caesar
Designer: Cathy Ryan
Mask maker: Paul Belmond

THE RITZ CINEMA

Gosport

The Ritz is a purpose built, 1930s cinema seating 1,200. It houses the largest screen on the south coast. Hampshire County Council asked AWA to investigate the feasibility of adding the facilities for live performances, while retaining the cinema. The project included extensive site surveys and market research. The design team aimed to retain the ambience of the building while adding the necessary performing space within the existing envelope. Catering and function facilities were added to enhance the venue's contribution to the town centre precinct.

Design consultants: Aveline Walne Associates, with
Jenny Lowe

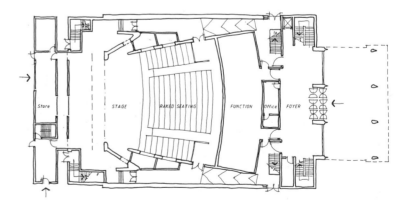

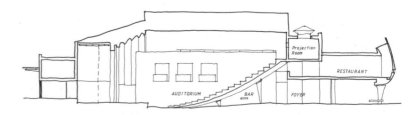

THE OLD FIRE STATION

Oxford

Martin McCallum: 'Rather than design a space and then superimpose the technical and practical needs of a theatre, in the case of The Old Fire Station the two were conceived as one. This duality was applied in the design of all aspects including the adjustable and motorised grids, incorporating cable ways, integral tracking and suspension systems; the flexible seating layout and the configuration of acoustic panels, Uni Strut fixing positions on the auditorium walls and the integral tracking and lighting positions on the leading edges of the galleries.'

Theatre design: Martin McCallum for the Mackintosh Foundation

MOBY DICK – A WHALE OF A TALE

Robert Longden and Hereward Kaye

Cameron Mackintosh Ltd, October 1991

Paul Farnsworth: 'The Old Fire Station itself dictated the design of the show – the audience is close to and part of the action. The response both it and the piece demanded was to dress the entire space with a mad assemblage of school and nautical items, reflecting the twin themes of schoolgirls and whaling. The aim was to create in the audience a feeling of excitement and expectation.'

Director: Robert Longden
Designer: Paul Farnsworth
Costume designer: Howard Rayner
Lighting designers: Howard Harrison and Hugh Vanstone
Choreographer: Anthony Lapsley

DONMAR WAREHOUSE

Covent Garden, London, reopened 1992

Nicholas Thompson (architect): 'The Donmar has a rich history, evident in the stone-flagged floor surviving from its days as a brewery stable and revealed in its layers of crumbling theatrical paintwork. It is into this 'found' space that the new Donmar Theatre has been inserted. Evolving through several formats, the spirit of the auditorium has been inherited, recalling the much loved natural and artless character of the original theatre. The rough, painted walls, the rawness of the steel and the robust timber screens recall a past while seeking to evoke a broader cultural context. The auditorium is capable of radical transformation and multiple interpre-tation at the hand of the Donmar's chosen designers. The basis for this freedom is the studied neutrality which is the essence of the auditorium design.'

Architects: RHWL Partnership Architects
Artistic director: Sam Mendes
Photo credit: John Walsom

NEW MUSICAL THEATRE

Duisburg, Germany, due for completion 1995

Nicholas Thompson: 'The New Musical Theatre is the latest in a series of projects in which RHWL has joined the design team at the request of Cameron Mackintosh Ltd, to create the interior design of the auditorium. The Duisburg Theatre continues and illustrates a thematic development of the reinter-pretation of the theatrical decorative tradition. A new structure carrying side boxes and creating an implied ceiling is overlaid with layers of vibrantly painted perforated metals and theatrical gauze. The audience is partially aware of the technology that creates the production and partially unaware, seduced by the undulating decorative surfaces.'

Architects: RHWL Partnership Architects

THESE IMAGES HAVE BEEN SPONSORED BY RHWL
PARTNERSHIP ARCHITECTS

Events and Non-theatre Performances

The reaction against formalised performance spaces may be either Romantic, political or pragmatic. In site-specific work, the environment, building or landscape becomes the basic setting and the driving force of the event. The design often blurs into the performance to determine the use of the space and the audience too becomes part of the performance. The scenic images are often symbols, icons or momentary spectacles and the use of bonfires, water and fireworks is common. This form of theatre is a fundamental aspect of community experience and celebration, whether it is high opera in an arena or a carnival procession.

Photo credit: Welfare State International

NIGHT SAFARI

**Secondary Forestation beside the
Seletar Reservoir, Singapore
Singapore Zoological Gardens, June 1994**

Simon Corder: 'Night Safari is the first night-time zoo in the world. Work commenced in 1988 and the gardens opened to the public in June 1994.

'Modern zoological design is essentially theatrical in its use of materials and attitude to space. Habitat simulation is the approach by which an animals' territory in the wild is reproduced to give visitors a chance to see the creature in context. The use of lighting, designed by a theatrical lighting designer, has helped to produce an extraordinary attraction. Night Safari sucks one into an enchanting nocturnal world, where nothing is what it seems.'

Designer: Simon Corder

FOOTFALLS

Samuel Beckett

**Garrick Theatre, London
March 1994**

Hildegard Bechtler: 'A 20-minute piece of theatre has to work viscerally and the experience has to be a totality. The foyers of the theatre were dismantled from their usual comforting purpose, the auditorium was disorientating, planks covered the stalls' plush seating, an abandoned platform hinted at a false focus of action and the stage lay bare except for a small light bulb, one of three that guided the viewers towards the action. The play proper started on the balcony, where the plaster work above the actress's head served as a ceiling for her perambulations, slightly crushing her head so she became a dangerous child in space, unable to find room, a mutation in shape as in life.'

Director: Deborah Warner
Designer: Hildegard Bechtler
Lighting designer: Jean Kalman
Photo credit: The Independent / Stuart Morris

STAIRWAY TO HEAVEN

Noel Greig and David Baird

**St Anne's Church Gardens, Soho
Shared Experience, July 1993**

Kate Owen: 'Dorothy L Sayers, writer of detective novels and translator of Dante, is buried in St Anne's churchyard along with thousands of victims of the plague. England does not have a history of joyous celebration of the dead and so I borrowed images from the Mexican Day of the Dead, and some Victorian and contemporary images. This piece of music theatre had almost 80 performers starting with a flame-lit street procession and ending with fireworks.'

Director: Luke Dixon
Designer: Kate Owen
Lighting designers: Luke Dixon and Jack Tilbury

A DREAM

Yazmine Judd

St Mark's Church, Silvertown, London
Theatre Venture, March 1994

Anthony Lamble: 'This was a community-based youth arts event. The company chose as a venue St Mark's, a disused, 19th-century church which had been at the heart of a Docklands community. Part of the brief was to create a complete theatre space comprising seating, lighting and dressing rooms. The set consisted of a series of circular stages in the body of the church punctuated by tall steel poles, a forest of real trees in the altar and chancel and a grey dissolving wall which divided the two areas. The materials reflected the wider environment: rusting steel poles, timber and real trees. Little was hidden. The church provided a beautiful and evocative backdrop.'

Directors: Jo Carter and John Riches
Set designer: Anthony Lamble
Costume designers: Anthony Lamble and Duggie Costain
Lighting designer: Simon Corder
Producer: Steve Moffitt

THE BURIAL OF THE DEAD

Devised, after T S Eliot

British Rail Paint Shed, Ashford
Ashford Youth Theatre, September 1991

Nigel Prabhavalkar: 'This was a collaborative work based on TS Eliot's *The Wasteland*. We chose this railway shed as it provided the environment we were seeking – with roller shutters, a crane and fearsome acoustics which we then integrated into the work. The set consisted of 42 tons of gravel, giving a suitable texture and sound. People and props emerged through this to tell stories and to create images of memories, birth and death. The image shows a moment from section three – *Memories*.'

Directors: Ramin Gray and Victoria Worsley
Designer: Nigel Prabhavalkar
Lighting designer: Charles Balfour
Sound designer: Laurence Muspratt

HAMLET
William Shakespeare

Open Air Theatre, Regents Park, London
New Shakespeare Company, June 1994

Tanya McCallin: 'The production was the first *Hamlet* in this open air space – a steeply raked amphitheatre facing an irregular shaped acting area, surrounded by tall trees. It had to play both in daylight and at night. The challenge was to brutalise the otherwise lyrical, pastoral space and to thrust forward the acting area, in order to focus this most complex, psychological drama. I wanted the set to relate organically with the space, yet to form a sharp, sculptural contrast. It is built of solid rusting steel with both large, curved and angular forms, allowing broad yet focused acting areas, with multiple exits and entrances. Costumes were inspired by the German Romantics, Liszt, Goethe and Caspar Friedrich.'

Director: Tim Pigott-Smith
Designer: Tanya McCallin
Lighting designer: Jason Taylor
Choreographer: Gillian Gregory

BEOWULF
Adapted by Michael Bogdanov

The Sugar Factory, Odense, Denmark
Odense Theater Company, March 1994

Claire Lyth: 'The director's brief explained: "Much of the script is illustrated narrative, therefore the visual emphasis should be on the actors, use of poles and silk to represent the ship, forest, river, cave, house, weapons and so on. We also need a back projection screen and a floor with a central padded area for fights."

'The Sugar Factory is an interesting space but not large. I put the BP screen in a triangular frame, partly to echo the apex of the roof, partly to get away from more conventional formats. The floor became radiating perspective floorboards with a central Celtic design painted on stretch fabric over judo mats. A Celtic border round the edge was surrounded by a black area for storing poles and props. For Act II we lost the screen to allow for the entrance of a huge dragon. The costumes were made of textured and interwoven strands of suede and leather; knitted leather represents chainmail. The idea was to create abstract warriors rather than realistic Vikings. Strips of fabric also became cloaks and sometimes props.'

Director: Michael Bogdanov
Designer: Claire Lyth
Lighting designer: Jens Klastrup

THE PIRATES OF PENZANCE
Gilbert and Sullivan

Valley Gardens, Saltburn
Cleveland Theatre Company, August 1992

Francis O'Connor: 'The solution to staging *Pirates* was almost immediate. The brief created the design: a cast of eight actors and five musicians performing out of doors. I created a huge packing crate which was opened up to reveal the ship for Act I. The cast was supplemented by the audience playing pirates and policemen and a lot of visible quick changes helped reveal new characters. In Act II the sail was lowered to reveal a painted graveyard with pop-up tombstones. I also gave the band a mini-crate to contain them and their instruments. The real beauty though was when closed, in crate form, it was completely secure from vandalism.'

Director: Alisdair Ramsey
Set designer: Francis O Connor
Lighting designer: Christopher Corner

TUTANKHAMUN
George Stiles and Anthony Drew

Imagination Atrium, London
Imagination Entertainments, November 1992

Peter Ruthven Hall: "A story that opens like Aladdin's cave and ends like a Greek myth of nemesis cannot fail to capture the imagination of all men and women," said Lady Burghclere.

'The headquarters of Imagination provided an extraordinary setting for this musical. The atrium became the Valley of the Kings by use of environmental projections on to the side walls; sand was spread across the floor under the seating and a night sky projected on to the canvas roof. The stairs from the ground floor conveniently became the stairs down into the tomb and the open bridges that crisscross the space were used for the scaffolding of the excavations, the press gallery in the courts, a balcony at Highclere Castle and by the spirits of Ancient Egypt. The ground floor and restaurant were dressed as the Metropolitan Museum in New York, complete with replica artefacts and security guards.'

Director: Andrew MacBean
Set and costume designer: Peter Ruthven Hall
Lighting designer: Jonathan Howard
Projection design: Kevin McKiernan
Audio visual supervisor: Chris Slingsby
Photo credit: Lisa Hooley

THE PERSIANS

Set model and mask and costume design for
Xerxes
Aeschylus, adapted by Howard Shaw

**The Grounds of Old St Chads, Shrewsbury,
August 1993**

Triadic: '*The Persians* was designed as an outdoor
touring production. The problem was to create a
concentrated environment suitable for a variety of
rural and urban settings. The solution was to use
three, large, semi-translucent banners to draw the
audience's attention to the performance and to
provide exits and entrances within an open space.
The director's concept was to use masks and
movement to present this very early text. The masks
and costumes were produced from an extensive
studio collaboration between director and designers.'

Director and choreographer: Howard Shaw
Set designer: Jeremy Longmore
Costume designer: Penny Wells
Mask designer: Jeremy Longmore

CARMINA BURANA
Carl Orff

Kings Hall, Belfast
Ulster Youth Dance, June 1991

Cecelia Doidge: 'The exhilerating spectacle of
Royston Maldoom's Carmina Burana inspired some
of Northern Ireland's professional musicians and
singers to join forces with the young dancers. The
entire Ulster Orchestra and the Belfast Philharmonic
Choir (about 350 singers) came together to create
one of the most complex and dramatic pieces of
staging and lighting ever seen.'

Choreographer: Royston Maldoom
Costume designer: Cecelia Doidge
Lighting designer: Peter Mumford

SPA

Treatment for a performance-installation, devised by Roger Bourke

Dartington Art Gallery, February 1995

Roger Bourke: 'Spa is a mix of a design-installation and live performance, intended for galleries and other non-theatre spaces. Through a variety of media it marries texts and a sound score, presented one-on-one, with a walk-through installation. It will open at Dartington Art Gallery in early 1995 and will subsequently tour to a number of venues in Britain and Europe.

'It is a part of the group of works which forms a project entitled Global Positioning. This examines some of the apparent disparities which exist in the way in which we live both physically and culturally in the final years of this century.

'The central image is of an operating fountain spouting a black liquid into a shallow square pool all within a misty space. Spa is concerned with the imagery of The Fountain and The Square which it adopts as Icons of Europe. It uses these to question our received attitudes towards health, sanity and cleanliness.'

TRIO IN E

Eric Rohmer and Wolfgang Amadeus Mozart

21 Royal Circus, Edinburgh
1st Framework Productions, September 1990

Peter Avery: 'A huge, elegant, first floor, domestic space was turned into the Parisian flat of a young composer to which an audience of 30 was invited each evening.'

Director: Peter Avery
Set designer: Laura Hopkins

THE ROYAL ALBERT HALL

A Season of 13 ballets in repertoire
The Bolshoi Ballet with Derek Block
International Concerts Limited
January 1993

Graham Walne: 'This image is an artist's impression of the Bolshoi stage inserted into the Royal Albert Hall. This presentation was believed to be the first to feature classical ballet on a thrust stage. The format presented a considerable technical challenge since the audience was seated where ballet side light is usually located. Additionally the repertoire and unpredictable rehearsal schedule demanded that the lighting could deliver any ballet at any moment.

'Valeri Leventhal's massive painted cloth stretching across the Albert Hall linked the Bolshoi auditorium perfectly with the Hall's boxes and provided a memorable setting. The cloth was lit to enhance the design; for example, 20 spotlights were focused to highlight the painted candelabra.'

Artistic director: Yuri Grigorovich
Designer of setting: Valeri Leventhal
Lighting designer: Graham Walne

TRAWLERS AT PEACE

Paedar Long and John Fox

Dockside, Grimsby
Welfare State International (with The Fishing Heritage Centre), October 1993

Welfare State International: 'Requiem – the occasion was the end of a very successful, long-running exhibition about the role of fishing in World War II.'

Director: Hilary Hughes
Set designers: Caroline Menis and Graeme Gilmour
Pyrotechnics: Mandy Dike
Photo credit: David Haley

THE MERCHANT OF VENICE

William Shakespeare

The Black Hills Playhouse, South Dakota
August 1994

Ralph Koltai: 'The Black Hills Playhouse is virtually at the foot of Mount Rushmore. Situated within a complex of timber barack huts, accommodating administration, cast, technicians, kitchen and dining hall it is distincly reminiscent of an army campsite in a forest clearing.

Director: Jan Swank
Designer: Ralph Koltai
Costume designer: Linda Wigley-Scribner
Lighting designer: Steve Thompson

LANTERN ARCADE

Daniel Fox

Tramway, Glasgow
Welfare State International (in collaboration with Roger Bloomfield and Caroline Scott)
December 1993

Performance Installation: Welfare State International

Director: John Fox
Set designers: Caroline Menis and Graeme Gilmour
Lighting designer: David Rennie
Photo credit: Kevin Low

FRAGILE GIFT

Daniel Fox

Old Fruit and Flower Market, Glasgow
Welfare State International, December 1992

Welfare State International: 'Occasion: alternative response to Christmas shopping commercialism as occurring in next door Candelriggs Market, Glasgow.'

Directors: Graeme Gilmour and Julian Crouch
Set designers: Welfare State International team
Lighting designers: Welfare State International team
Photo credit: Kevin Low

BIOGRAPHIES

JULIAN ADAMS
Julian Adams studied theatre design at Croydon, graduating in 1990. He has since worked as an assistant at the Thorndike Theatre, Leatherhead, the Queen's Theatre, Hornchurch and, for the past four years, has been responsible for designing the major productions at the Stag Theatre, Sevenoaks. These have included *The Matchgirls*, *A Man for All Seasons*, *La Cage aux Folles*, *Hans Andersen*, *Bugsy Malone* and *Camelot*. Other design credits include *Cabaret*, *Origin of the Species*, *La Traviata* and *Faust* for Surrey Opera.

CARLA EVE AMIE
Carla Eve Amie studied theatre design at Wimbledon School of Art (1986-87) and Trent Polytechnic (1988-91). In 1992 she was Arts Council Trainee in Theatre for Young People. She is committed to creating educational and issue-based theatre in which design refrains from rigid realism and stimulates emotion and discussion through the nature of the materials used. These include everyday objects such as plastic, hair, clothing and fencing used in an unconventional manner to create a new form or environment. Design work has included *Mixed Blessings*, a play on race relations and *No Mean Street* about HIV in the black community, for Red Ladder Theatre Company; *Shared Testament* , which looked at spirituality in contemporary society, for RJC Dance Theatre; *All's Well That Ends Well* and *Pericles*, both final year shows for Arden School of Theatre, Manchester and *The Petticoat Rebellion* about the birth of the suffrage movement, for the Italia Conti Academy. She has worked in youth theatre in Nottingham, Edinburgh and Belfast, run design workshops for Theatre Centre, Nottingham Playhouse, Roundabout TIE, schools and colleges, and teaches the Performing Arts Design Module to BTEC National Diploma level. She is a member of the Designers Formation Co-operative agency.

PAUL ANDREWS
Paul Andrews trained at the Wimbledon School of Art and Design. His designs have included *Romeo and Juliet* for Sir Kenneth Macmillan and the Birmingham Royal Ballet; West Side Story for the Cambridge Festival and tour; *All's Well That Ends Well* and *The Rivals* with Helena Kaut Howson and Caroline Eves for Theatre Clwyd; *The Taming of the Shrew*, *The Merchant of Venice* and *Gypsy* for Jude Kelly at West Yorkshire Playhouse. Current contracts include *Cheriomushki* with Lucy Bailey at the Lyric Theatre, Hammersmith; *Mail Order Bride* and *The Sound of Music* at West Yorkshire Playhouse.

SARAH ASHPOLE
Sarah Ashpole trained at the Wimbledon School of Art from 1984-87. She won second prize in the Linbury Prize for Stage Design for *The Turn of The Screw*. She was assistant designer to Nigel Lowery on *The Fall of the House of Usher* at the Queen Elizabeth Hall, London, *The Plumber's Gift* and *Die Fledermaus* for English National Opera, and *The Gondoliers* for the D'Oyly Carte Opera Company.

Designs have included *The Three Sisters* and *Trojan Women* (Old Vic Youth Theatre at the Jeanetta Cochrane Theatre); *Dido and Aeneas* (Welsh National Opera and the Sherman Theatre, Cardiff); Offenbach's *Monsieur Choufleuri* (WNO education department); *Master Peter's Puppets* by de Falla (National Youth Music Theatre at the Edinburgh Festival, Covent Garden piazza and St John's, Smith Square); *Cosi Fan Tutte* for the British Youth Opera on tour; *Othello* at Emmanuel College, Cambridge; *Fate – La Forza del Destino* for Scottish Opera at the Tron Theatre, Glasgow; *A Room with a View* for Snap People's Theatre Trust at the Yvonne Arnaud Theatre, Guildford; *Crimes of Love* for Trestle Theatre Company at the Queen Elizabeth Hall; *The Marriage of Figaro* for the Opera Company; *The Provok'd Wife* at the New End, Hampstead *Gaslight* at the Northcott Theatre, Exeter; Monteverdi's *Orfeo* at Birmingham Conservatoire; and *Dawnpath* by Nicola LeFanu at the Sherman Theatre, Cardiff.

AVELINE WALNE ASSOCIATES
Aveline Walne Associates (AWA) is a theatre design and management consultancy formed in 1992 by Joe Aveline and Graham Walne. Associates include architectural designer Jenny Lowe BSc, AA Dipl. and quantity surveyor Michael Porter FRICS.

The two partners have over 60 years' experience in the production and management of the arts and arts organisations. Aveline is a former general manager of the Institute of Contemporary Arts, London and Walne completed 50 projects through his consultancy company, Leisureplan, before forming AWA. Both partners continue to work as designers and production managers giving them an informed insight into the minutiae of both front-of-house and backstage operations. Recent projects have included feasibility studies, safety audits and organisational reviews. Clients have included Hampshire County Council, Southern Arts Board, the Manoel Theatre, Malta, the district councils of Salisbury, Eastleigh, Fareham, Torbay and Restormel, and the city council of Southampton.

SUE AYERS
Sue Ayers trained at the Arts Educational School and the Central St Martin's School of Art and Design, where she designed the costumes for the opera *One Man Show* which opened The Jeannetta Cochrane Theatre. She has worked as a costume designer with Sean Kenny; she consulted JB Priestley about her design for Bernard Miles' production of *An Inspector Calls* at The Mermaid Theatre, London; she has designed and co-produced a touring production of *A Kurt Weill Cabaret* with David Raphael and designed *Gertrude Stein and a Companion* for Miriam Margolyes at the Edinburgh Festival.

She has been a visiting lecturer at Camberwell School of Art for 15 years where, under Joe Dixon, she has continued her own artistic education. She is a member of Just Art, a fine art group producing paintings, decorated ceramics and handmade books.

RICHARD AYLWIN
Richard Aylwin studied fine art, specialising in sculpture. He works as an artist and designer for theatre and opera companies and with community development programmes for various arts organisations such as Opera North, English National Opera, Scottish Chamber Orchestra and London Symphony Orchestra. Recent designs for theatre have included *The Rising of the Moon* at Wexford Festival Opera; *The Shaming of Bright Millar* at Contact Theatre; *Who's Afraid of Virginia Woolf* at the Cheltenham Everyman; and a new production of *Katya Kabanova* for Scottish Opera.

ZOE BACHARACH
Zoe Bacharach studied Theatre Design at Croydon College. Designs have included *Noye's Fludde* at Andover Festival; *Blithe Spirit* for Mayfly at the Oxford Union; *Free Spirit* for Shared Experience Youth Theatre; *Lipstick Dreams* at Greenwich Studio Theatre; *The Island* by Athol Fugard for African Reflections; and *Dante's Inferno* for Kazzum at the Edinburgh Fringe Festival. She has also worked as a freelance prop maker and scene painter.

She spent two years as associate resident designer at the New Victoria Theatre in North Staffordshire. There she collaborated with Peter Cheeseman on *Turkey Time*, *The Plough and the Stars*, *Relatively Speaking* and *Nice Girls*. She designed *Too*, *Eric the Epic*, *Buddy's Song* and *C'mon Stan* with Rob Swain and *Les Liaisons Dangereuses* with Bob Eaton.

MARTYN BAINBRIDGE
Martyn Bainbridge's theatre designs include productions at the Theatre Royal, Plymouth of *A Little Night Music*, *The Birthday Party*, *Kes*, *My Cousin Rachel*, *Outside Edge*, *Pump Boys and Dinettes*, *Absurd Person Singular*, *Charley's Aunt*, *The Shadow of a Gunman*, *I Have Been Here Before* and the national tour of *Master Forger*.

Other designs have included *Measure for Measure* at Nye Theater, Oslo; *Deathtrap* at the Northcott Theatre, Exeter; *Outside Edge* at the Churchill Theatre, Bromley, *Shakespeare's Double* for the RSC at the Other Place; *The Soldier's Tale* at the Oxford Playhouse and *On The Razzle* at West Yorkshire Playhouse.

Recent opera designs have included *Ariadne auf Naxos* at Garsington Opera, *The Trial* at the Collegiate Theatre, London; *Die Zauberflöte* for Kent Opera; *Madama Butterfly* for Phoenix Opera; *Norma* and *La Traviata* for Northern Ireland Opera; *La Rondine* at the Royal Academy of Music; *Le Nozze di Figaro* at the Guildhall School of Music and Drama and *Béatrice et Benédict* for Indianapolis Opera. His ballet designs include *Daphnis et Chloé* for The Royal Ballet at Covent Garden.

Designed exhibitions have included *The Astronomes* at the London Planetarium; *Armada 1588-1988* at the National Maritime Museum, Greenwich, *Lawrence of Arabia* at the National Portrait Gallery; London, and *Daendels* at the Rijksmuseum, Amsterdam. He also designed the permanent exhibition for Madame Tussaud's in Amsterdam, *Madame Tussaud Scenerama*.

ANTHONY BAKER
Anthony Baker trained at the Central School of Art, London. He has designed for opera, both in the United Kingdom and internationally. His work has included *Faust* for New Sussex Opera; *Angelique*, *La Vida Breve*, *La Colombe* and *L'Heure Espagnole* for Guildhall School of Music and Drama; *Die Zauberflöte* for Opera '80 on tour; *The Black Spider* by Judith Weir for Buxton Festival; *The Jewel Box* by Mozart for Opera North and Glyndebourne; *Cosi Fan Tutte* and *Don Pasquale* for Welsh National Opera; *Cosi Fan Tutte* for Seattle Opera, USA and *Una Cosa Rara* at Drottningholm Court Theatre, Stockholm. He has co-directed and designed *Le Nozze di Figaro* for Surrey Opera.

Most recently he designed Handel's *Giulio Cesare in Egitto* for Australian Opera at the Sydney Opera House. Plans include a revival of *Cosi Fan Tutte*, directed by Tim Hopkins for Welsh National Opera opening in May 1995.

TONY BANFIELD
Tony Banfield studied at Camberwell Art School and worked for some years as a graphic artist specialising in architectural perspective illustration. In 1978 he joined the one-year postgraduate course in Theatre Design at Croydon College where he discovered skills in scene painting and model making. Following this he was awarded an Arts Council Bursary to work for a year at the Redgrave Theatre where he designed six productions.

For Theatre Powys he designed a range of work from *Twelfth Night* to *Pinnochio*, from *Sinbad* in-the-round to *Quasimodo*, designed for performance in castle courtyards. For Theatre of Thelema he created a series of highly technical, compact touring shows for children for which he had to adapt many traditional stage mechanisms to unusual situations.

He also works as a scene painter and since 1991 has been part-time tutor at Croydon College. In the past few years he has revived a childhood preoccupation with model theatres. He has produced a limited edition of 1:25 scale models, based on the Old Vic Theatre, which are much in demand and which have opened up a whole new sphere of work.

SIMON BANHAM
Born in Nigeria, Simon Banham studied Fine Art in Newcastle and Theatre Design in Cardiff at the Sherman Theatre. Since then he has designed for opera, music theatre and theatre companies around the country and abroad. Notable productions include *The Threepenny Opera* (Welsh National Opera); *The Country Wife* (York Theatre Royal); *Il Seraglio* (Opera 80); *The Feast of the Pheasant* (Tramway, Glasgow); *La Fiercilla Domada* (Murcia, Spain); the premiere of Stephen Oliver's *Euridice* (Music Theatre Wales); *Gli Ingannati* (Sienna, Italy); the world premiere of Andrew Toovey's opera *Ubu* (Banff, Canada); *The Tempest* (Londrina Festival, Brazil) and *The Lighthouse* (Music Theatre Wales in Stuttgart, Germany).

Since coming to Contact Theatre as resident designer Simon has designed *The Threepenny Opera*, *The Adventures of Tom Sawyer*, *Dracula*, *Doctor Faustus*, the English premiere of *Mary Queen of Scots Got Her Head Chopped Off*, the world premiere of *The Singing Ringing Tree*, *Measure for Measure*, *The Seagull*, Bryan Elsley's *Elidor*, *Surface Tension* (a co-production with Gregory Nash) and the world premiere production of *The Carver Chair*. Most recently he has designed *Lysistrata* for Contact Theatre and *The Idol on the Bronze Horse*, a co-production between Contact Theatre and the Palace of Youth Creativity in St Petersburg, Russia.

HILARY BAXTER

Hilary Baxter studied theatre design at the Central School of Art and Design. She currently lectures in costume design at the Wimbledon School of Art. For the past nine years she has worked for many different companies in fringe, community, repertory and national theatres. Credits include the set and costume designs for *The Mistress* (Teatro Fliano, Rome); *Good Sisters* (Crucible Theatre) and *Pericles* (Cambridge Arts Theatre). Her most recent commission was the design of the costumes for *Torquato Tasso*, translated and directed by Robert David MacDonald (Edinburgh Festival, 1994)

HILDEGARD BECHTLER

Hildegard Bechtler was born in Stuttgart, lives and works in London. She trained at Camberwell and Central St. Martin's Schools of Art. She made her theatre debut at the ICA with *Ella* by Herbert Achternbusch, directed by Tim Albery. She designed several productions at the Almeida Theatre including Botho Strauss' *Tourist Guide* and *The Saxon Shore* by David Rudkin; she also made her opera debut there with *Jacob Lenz* by Wolfgang Riehm. During this time she worked very closely with director Pierre Audi and lighting designer Jean Kalman.

Recent opera includes *La Wally* by Alfredo Catalini (Bregenz and Netherlands Opera) directed by Tim Albery for whom she also designed the sets for *Peter Grimes* (ENO and Munich Staatsoper), *Lohengrin* (English National Opera) and *Don Carlos* (Opera North); and also *Bacchae* (ENO).

In theatre she has worked mostly with the director Deborah Warner on productions of *Electra* (Royal Shakespeare Company, Riverside Studios and Boubigny, Paris); *King Lear* (Royal National Theatre and world tour); *Hedda Gabler*, winner of the 1992 Olivier Award Best Production (Abbey Theatre, Dublin and The Playhouse, London); *Coriolanus* (Salzburg); and Beckett's *Footfalls* (Garrick Theatre, London). They have also collaborated on two opera productions, Alban Berg's *Wozzeck* (Opera North) and *Don Giovanni* (Glyndebourne Festival Opera).

Production design credits for film and television include *Business as Usual*, *Coming up Roses*, *The Bad Sister*, *Sacred Hearts*, *Echoes* and more recently *Hedda Gabler* and *Peter Grimes* for the BBC. She is currently designing the sets for *Simon Boccanegra* for Munich Staatsoper (1995).

KATE BORTHWICK

Kate Borthwick trained at Wimbledon School of Art. She recently designed *Desperate Journey* and *As You Like It* for TAG Theatre Company, Glasgow which toured widely to venues across Scotland from the Citizen's Theatre, Glasgow, and the Traverse, Edinburgh, to Kirkwell Arts Theatre, Orkney and the Garrison Theatre, Shetland.

In Scotland she has also worked with Wiseguise, Arches Theatre and Dundee Repertory Dance Company, designing pieces such as *Vinegar and Brown Paper*, Ionesco's *Rhinoceros*, Tony Harrison's *V*, *The Caretaker* by Harold Pinter and *Hughie on the Wires* by Donal O'Kelly.

Her other work includes *Alice in Wonderland – The Opera* (Harrogate International Opera Festival) and Handel's *Semele* (New Athenaeum, Glasgow); art direction on *The Catch* (Edinburgh Film Festival, 1993); scene painting for Naked Films on the feature film *Vampire* and various pop promos.

She has wide experience of design in contemporary dance and has worked with choreographers including David Dorfman on *Him* (Digital Dance Award commission) and Janet Smith on *Tam Lin* (1993 Mayfest production). In 1989 she was one of the founders of D-Note Dance Co. She was props co-ordinator and performer with the Manchester-based company Dogs of Heaven for its site-specific performance of *Safe as Houses* in the Crescents, Hulme 1993.

ROGER BOURKE

Roger Bourke has worked as an artist and designer in theatre for a number of years. This has included a period during the 1970s in theatre-in-education as Resident Designer for Greenwich Young People's Theatre. He has also devised and designed large-scale, site-specific events in Britain and France.

During the 1980s he was particularly concerned with designing for new writing. This included a long association with writer Stephen Lowe for whom he designed *Tibetan Inroads* (Royal Court) and *Strive, Desire and Demon Lovers* (Meeting Ground Theatre Co.). He has worked with director Annie Castledine on designs for *Translations* by Brian Friel (Theatre Clwyd) and *Tokens of Affection* by Maureen Lawrence (Derby Playhouse). His designs for *Tibetan Inroads* and *Translations* were included in the British entries to the Prague Quadrennial Exhibitions in 1983 and 1987.

Recent work has been concerned with forms of installation and new performance. He is currently director of the visual performance course at Dartington College of Arts.

JAN BEE BROWN

Jan Bee Brown started her career writing radio plays for All India Radio in the Himalayas, and graduated in theatre design from the Central School of Art and Design in 1985. She continued her apprenticeship at the Abbey Theatre in Dublin where she became a resident designer in 1987, designing *Purple Dust*, *The Glass Menagerie*, *Hughie* and a season of new plays by Irish writers. She has since worked freelance in opera and dance in Britain, Germany and India. Opera work includes *Il Tabarro* and *Suor Angelica* by Puccini, the world premiere of *Nell by Bawd* (Donmar Warehouse) and Handel's *Agrippina* (Midsummer Opera). Her dance work includes *Under The Moon*, *Kali Yug* and *Changing Planes* (Pan Projects). In 1991, she designed *Hobson's Choice* for the Derby Playhouse which won the TMA Award for Best Overall Production and more recently she designed the acclaimed new musical, *A Christmas Carol* for Theatr Clwyd. She is Resident Designer at the Stephen Joseph Theatre and has designed both last and this summer's season of plays at the studio and the recent main house productions of *Physical Jerks*, *Love Off The Shelf*, *Mr A's Amazing Maze Plays*, *The End of the Food Chain*, *Haunting Julia*, *Gaslight* and *Penny Blue*.

JOHANNA BRYANT

Johanna Bryant trained in theatre design at Hereford and at Wimbledon School of Art under the tuition of Richard Negri. She has designed productions all over the country and was resident designer for the '69' Theatre Company for three years before it became the Royal Exchange Theatre Company.

For the Royal Exchange she has designed *The Rivals*, *The Gentle People*, *Leaping Ginger*, *The Three Musketeers*, *Have you Anything to Declare?*, *Measure for Measure*, *Blood Black and Gold*, *Waiting for Godot*, *The Beaux Stratagem*, Andy Capp, *The Nerd*, *The Government Inspector*, *Hamlet*, *Cat on a Hot Tin Roof*, *The Admirable Crichton*, *Long Day's Journey into Night*, *Riddley Walker*, *Oedipus*, *Twelfth Night*, *Macbeth*, *The Odd Couple*, *The Tempest*, *Your Home in the West*, *Doctor Heart*, *The Recruiting Officer*, *The Odd Women*, and the sets for *The Bluebird of Unhappiness* and *The Cabinet Minister*

Most recently she designed the set and costumes for two world premieres: Ronald Harwood's *Poison Pen* and Mikhail Shatrov's *Maybe*. She has designed productions for the Edinburgh and Ludlow Festivals, Rambert Dance Company and the Shaw Theatre Company.

DAVID BUCKLAND

David Buckland is both a designer and an artist. He has designed over 20 sets and costumes mainly for dance and ballet companies. His work has been commissioned by Rambert Dance Company, Siobhan Davies Dance Company, English National Ballet, Second Stride and the French Compagnie Cre-Ange. Recently he has worked on the opera *The Man with the Wind at his Heels* (ENO/Almeida Theatre). Five of his designs have been re-worked for film and have been broadcast on British television.

As an artist he has exhibited in numerous galleries in London, Paris and New York and his work has been bought by the National Portrait Gallery, London, the Centre Georges Pompidou, Paris, the Metropolitan Museum, New York and the Getty Museum, Los Angeles. His most recent exhibition was at the Zwemmer Gallery in London. Three books of his work have been published.

KATE BURNETT

Kate Burnett trained at Ravensbourne, West Sussex and Croydon and now lives in Manchester. She has designed for theatre since 1978, working extensively in repertory, touring, and theatre-in-education

Most recently she designed *B-Road Movie* (Lipservice); *Mother Courage and Her Children* and *The Day After Tomorrow* for four to seven year-olds (Royal National Theatre and tour).

She was Head of Design at Contact Theatre and won the Manchester Evening News Design Award for an entire season's work in 1986-87. Her productions there between 1985-1989 included *The Snowman* (also seen at Leicester Haymarket), *The Little Prince*, *To Kill a Mocking Bird* (also Greenwich Theatre), *Female Parts*, *Mother Courage*, and *The Duchess of Malfi*. Other designs have included *Doctor Faustus* (Young Vic), which won a Time Out Design Award, *Brighton Rock* (West Yorkshire Playhouse); *Of Mice and Men*, *Macbeth*, and *The Threepenny Opera* (Birmingham Rep). For the National Theatre of Brent, she designed *The Complete Guide To Sex* (Lyric Hammersmith) and *Mighty Moments in World History* (also seen on Channel 4). She designed the original production of *Return to the Forbidden Planet* (London Bubble Theatre).

Since receiving an Arts Council Bursary in 1989, Kate Burnett has worked as an artist-in-education for the Whitechapel and Cornerhouse Galleries, and in schools. She devised the education programme for the Manchester International Festival of Expressionism in 1992. In the aftermath of this she started to develop the theatre design exhibition which has become *Make Space!*

DAVID BURROWS

David Burrows has worked with director Phil Young for ten years on productions including *Crystal Clear* (Wyndhams Theatre), *Les Miroirs Brises* (French Institute), *The Train Years* (MOMI), *Knickers* (Lyric Hammersmith), *Blood Brothers* (Heilbronn, Germany), and *Tonight: Lola Blau* (Old Red Lion, Islington). Collaborations with director Alkis Kritikos have included *Miss Julie* (Sir Richard Steel Theatre, London), *The Collector* (Portlands Playhouse, London), the British premiere of Beckett's *Rough for Theatre 1 & 2* (Theatro Technis and national tour) and *In Other Beasts the Best* (Theatro Technis).

He is Principal Lecturer in the Theatre Department at Wimbledon School of Art and Course Leader of the technical arts, design and interpretation courses. In the formative years of its validation (1989 - 1994) he was also Course Leader of the country's first master course in theatre design/scenography.

Stimulated by their work in theatre and higher education but dismayed at the increasingly difficult professional context facing new graduates in the performing arts, David Burrows and theatre director Jonathan Martin have launched the *Gangway Directory* which will detail the whereabouts, skills and aspirations of subscribing new graduates (from 1995 and annually thereafter) from the UK's performing arts courses, the aim being to empower new theatre practitioners by providing a networking resource and means to build new interdisciplinary enterprises.

JOHN BURY

John Bury was educated at Hereford Cathedral School and University College, London. After serving in the Royal Navy during World War II he joined Joan Littlewood's Theatre Workshop as an actor, but was quickly transferred to the technical departments. He spent his early years as a stage hand, stage manager and electrician. By the mid 1950s he was designing lighting and sets.

In 1958, he was Principal Designer at the Theatre Royal, Stratford East and designed Shelagh Delaney's *A Taste of Honey*, Brendan Behan's *The Quare Fellow*, Lionel Bart's *Fings Ain't Wot They Used to Be*, and Joan Littlewood's *Oh! What a Lovely War!* In 1962 he joined Peter Hall's Royal Shakespeare Theatre at Stratford-upon-Avon. Here, after three years as Associate Designer he became the company's first Head of Design, a post he held until 1968. He designed most of the major Shakespeare plays, including *The Wars of the Roses Cycle*, the *Quatrocentenary History Cycle* (*Richard II* to *Richard III* inclusive), *Hamlet*, *Macbeth*, *Coriolanus*, *Henry VIII* and (twice) *Measure for Measure*.

John Bury designed the first production of Harold Pinter's *The Collection* and most other first productions of Pinter's work including *The Homecoming*, *Landscape*, *Silence*, *Old Times*, *No Man's Land* and *The Betrayal*. From 1968 to 1973 he was a freelance designer working mainly in opera. In New York he designed *The Rothschilds*, the ill-fated *Via Galactica*, *The Doll's House* and *Hedda Gabler* and in Tokyo, *Hamlet* and *Phaedra*. In 1973 he joined Peter Hall again at the National Theatre, where he was appointed Head of Design, a post he held until 1985. During this period he designed ten operas for Glyndebourne Festival Opera.

He now works mainly in opera, both in Europe and the USA, until recently designing two or three operas a year. He works in close collaboration with his wife Elizabeth Bury, who bears an ever increasing and important share of the creative responsibilities.

ISABELLA BYWATER

In 1987 Isabella Bywater designed the award-winning production of *Titus Andronicus* for the Royal Shakespeare

Company, first at the Swan Theatre then at The Pit in London. In 1989 it toured to Madrid, Paris, Copenhagen and Denmark.

Her opera credits include *The Flying Dutchman*, *The Turn of the Screw*, *Nabucco*, *The Barber of Seville*, *Eugene Onegin*, *Il Trittico*, *The Snow Queen* and *The Marriage of Figaro*. She made her Swedish debut with *Hello Dolly* (Musikteater I Varmland). She also designed a major new musical, *La Belle Epoque* (Stockholm); *The Duenna*, *The Merry Wives of Windsor* and *La Finta Giardiniera* (Guildhall School of Music and Drama); *Cav and Pag* (Stockholm), *Madam Butterfly* (Mid Wales Opera) and *L'Elisir D'Amore* (English Touring Opera).

Recent theatre designs include *Heaven* (Bristol Express at the Lillian Baylis Theatre, London), *Woman in Mind*, costumes for *Jack and the Beanstalk*, *A Midsummer Night's Dream*, *The Doll's House*, *All My Sons*, *School for Wives* and *The Tempest* (Salisbury Playhouse); and *Of Mice and Men* (Nottingham Playhouse).

ALISON CHITTY

Alison Chitty trained at St Martin's School of Art (Foundation) and at Central School of Art and Design (Theatre Design), London. She went on to design over 40 productions at the New Victoria Theatre, in North Staffordshire, as well as *Uncle Vanya* (Hampstead Theatre); *Measure for Measure* and *Julius Caesar* (Riverside Studios); *Carmen Jones* and *Lennon* (Sheffield Crucible and West End). Other designs include *Tartuffe*, *Volpone*, *Breaking the Silence* and *Romeo and Juliet* (Royal Shakespeare Company).

She was Resident Designer at the Royal National Theatre for eight years, where her work included *A Month in the Country*, *Don Juan*, *Much Ado About Nothing*, *The Prince of Homburg*, *Danton's Death*, *Major Barbara*, *Kick for Touch*, *Venice Preserv'd*, (British Drama Award), *Tales from Hollywood*, *Antigone* and *Fool for Love*, (which transferred to the West End). She received an Olivier nomination for *She Stoops to Conquer* and *Martine*. She also designed Peter Hall's productions of *Antony and Cleopatra* and *The Tempest*. Other work in the West End includes *Orpheus Descending* (Haymarket and Neil Simon Theatre, Broadway) and *Rose Tattoo* (Playhouse).

Alison Chitty has designed several operas including *The Marriage of Figaro* (Opera North); *New Year* (Houston Grand Opera and Glyndebourne); *Gawain* (Royal Opera House); *L'Assedio di Calais* (Wexford Festival); *The Vanishing Bridegroom* (Opera Theatre, St Louis); *Falstaff* (Gotenburg Music Theatre, Sweden); *Jenufa* (Dallas Opera); *Billy Budd* (Geneva) and *Blond Eckbert* (Santa Fe). She is currently preparing *Khovanshchina* (English National Opera), *Modern Painters* (Santa Fe) and *Arianna* (Royal Opera House).

Film work includes *Blue Jean* (David Bowie Video), *Life is Sweet* (Mike Leigh), *Black Poppies* (BBC), *A Sense of History* (C4) and *Naked* (Mike Leigh).

She is Co-Director of the one-year post-graduate Motley Theatre Design Course.

DAVID COCKAYNE

David Cockayne trained at Birmingham College of Art. He has designed for, amongst others, Brimingham Repertory Theatre, Liverpool Playhouse, Manchester Library Theatre Company, Theatre Clwyd, Leicester Haymarket Studio. Leeds Playhouse, Sheffield Crucible, Great Eastern Stage and the Cheltenham Everyman Theatre.

Work with Manchester Library Theatre Company has included *Richard II*, *Sell-Out*; *Volpone*; *Julius Ceasar*; *The Ruling Class*; *When The Actors Come* and pantomimes. For Leeds Playhouse he has designed *The Devil's Disciple*; *Masterpieces*; *Passion Play* and *Scenes from a Voyage to the Indies*. Designs for the Cheltenham Everyman have included *When We Are Married*; *Jack and the Beanstalk* and *Leave Him to Heaven*. Recent work has included *The Two Lockets*, a young persons' opera (Sheffield Crucible Studio) and *Retreat from Moscow* (New End Theatre, London). His work includes theatre photography and since 1980 he has lectured in theatre design at Nottingham Trent University.

ROSEMARIE COCKAYNE

As a child, Rosemarie Cockayne was taught mime by the legendary Ballerina from the Diaghilev Ballet, Tamara Karsavina, whose spirit she remembers clearly – warmth, gentleness and dignity. These qualities were shown again by the teacher recommended to her by Madame Karsavina – Stanislas Idzikowski – also a great name in the Ballet Russes.

Following this training and whilst continuing to study at her day school, she went to the Royal Ballet Senior School and worked with Peter Brinson and Ballet for All. She left the Royal Ballet School to become a soloist and then a season later she became Ballerina, dancing the classics, with Waslav Orlikowsky at the Basle State Ballet. It was during her time as Ballerina in Switzerland that she started painting, inspired by the strong colours of the Expressionists. She now works in a variety of media from pen and charcoal line-drawing to bold use of expressionistic colour.

Returning to London she danced and painted before deciding to concentrate on painting. She has exhibited her work internationally and there are collections of her work in various locations including the headquarters of IBM, the Clydesdale Bank, Sheraton Park Tower Hotel and University College Hospital. She has produced designs for company logos and is also involved as a stage designer, creating sets and costumes for *Nutcracker*, *Coppelia* and *Jazz Ballet*.

TREVOR COE

Trevor Coe trained at Newcastle College of Art and Industrial Design and Trent Polytechnic in the Department of Theatre Design. His first professional work was as a design technician for the Newcastle University Theatre (now Tyneside Theatre Company) and he started designing for the company's young persons theatre wing, Stagecoach. After a four-year apprenticeship and, with some main house designs to his credit, he moved to Chester where he took up the position of Resident Designer with the touring group attached to Chester Arts Centre.

In 1979 he became Head of Design for the Gateway Theatre, Chester. After four seasons and having designed sets and costumes for over 24 productions for them, he became resident Head of Design at Pitlochry Festival Theatre. Nine seasons and 49 sets later, he has stepped down but maintains a close relationship with the company. Freelance work has included designs for companies such as Bristol Old Vic, Windsor Theatre Royal, Leicester Phoenix, Coventry Belgrade and Perth Theatre.

KEN COKER

Ken Coker started his lighting career at the Arts Theatre Cambridge where he lit the *Footlights' Review*. Since then his lighting career has encompassed everything from lighting the Hank Wangford Band – under the *nomme de guerre* Brent Cross – to lighting *Island to Island* for Rambert Dance company. Recently he has lit *Macbeth* for the English Shakespeare Company Education Department, *The Sum of Us* (The Warehouse, Croydon) and *Elegies for Angels, Punks and Raging Queens* (Criterion Theatre, London). Outside London he has lit *Brighton Rock* (West Yorkshire Playhouse) and *Cinderella* by Peter Maxwell Davies (Aldeburgh Foundation Education Department).

He was lighting designer for the British premiere of *Closer than Ever* for Crusaid and is currently busy on a variety of projects some of which are part of the City of Drama celebrations.

PATRICK CONNELLAN

Patrick Connellan won the Linbury Prize for Stage Design in 1987 and has since worked extensively around the country. In 1989 he designed the indoor production of Wagner's *The Flying Dutchman* (Bregenzer Festspiele). Recent productions include *Misery* (Criterion Theatre, Piccadilly, and national tour); *Cider with Rosie*, *The Pied Piper*, *The Grapes of Wrath*, *Nervous Women*, *The Atheist's Tragedy* and *Rough* (Birmingham Rep); *When We Are Married* and *The Rivals* (West Yorkshire Playhouse); *Time And The Conways* (Octagon Theatre, Bolton); *Misery* (Leicester Haymarket); and *A Passionate Woman* (Comedy Theatre, London).

KANDIS COOK

Kandis Cook trained on the Motley Theatre Design Course when it was based at English National Opera and at the Nova Scotia College of Fine Art.

She has recently completed costume designs for Matthew Warchus' production of *Henry V* for the Royal Shakespeare Company. Other work includes *Women Beware Women*, *The Grace of Mary Traverse* and *The Faith Healer* (Royal Court); *The Crucible* (Leicester Haymarket); *Hamlet* (Donmar Warehouse and Piccadilly Theatre); *Britannicus*, *Berenice*, *The Relapse* (Lyric, Hammersmith) and *Dr Faustus* (Lyric Hammersmith and Fortune Theatre); *Love's Labours Lost* and *Richard II* (Royal Exchange Theatre, Manchester); *Arden of Faversham*, *The Bite of the Night*, *The Silent Woman*, *The Last Days of Don Juan* (Royal Shakespeare Company); *Orlando* (Wexford Festival Opera) and the realisation of Gerald Scarfe's costume designs for *Orpheus in the Underworld* (English National Opera).

SIMON CORDER

Simon Corder began his theatrical career as a ring boy in a circus. He joined Lumiere & Son in 1981 as their technical director, set and lighting designer. Among the 20 productions staged in theatres, parks, tents, Nottingham Castle and a swimming pool in Penzance, he designed the lighting for *Deadwood* (Royal Botanical Gardens, Kew) and *Paradise* (UK tour).

As a freelance lighting designer since 1987 he has worked in avant-garde and middle-scale theatre, opera, dance and performance. Productions have included the premiere production of Judith Weir's opera *The Vanishing Bridegroom* (Scottish Opera); *Cosi Fan Tutte* (Welsh National Opera); *Orpheus in the Underworld* (Opera North); *Carmen* (Tanz-Forum at Oper der Stadt, Cologne); *Hippolytos* (Almeida Theatre, London) and *The Destiny of Me* (Leicester Haymarket).

As a photographer he has produced images for projection, news and arts features, notably *Hippies at Stonehenge* (National Trust Press Office); *Panic* (Lumiere & Son, European Tour); *The London Project* (Photographers Gallery, London) and *The Planets Suite* (Ulster Orchestra).

As a lighting design consultant he has produced reports and proposals for theatre companies, arts centres and outdoor lighting projects. He has recently completed an installation of over 40 hectares of *Night Safari* for the Singapore Zoological Gardens; the first simulated habitat to reproduce an animal's territory in the wild to give visitors a chance to see 1200 creatures in context.

SALLY CRABB

Sally Crabb started her theatrical career at Phoenix Arts, Leicester where she designed some 25 productions. She then went to the Victoria Theatre, Stoke before joining the Oldham Coliseum.

She designed Brecht's *Life of Galileo* (Bristol Old Vic), *Our Town* (Contact Theatre, Manchester), *Le Misanthrope* (Cambridge Theatre Company) and *Uncle Vanya* (Gate Theatre, Dublin). In 1986 she became Head of Design at the Bristol Old Vic where, among other productions, she designed *Intimate Exchanges*, *The Cherry Orchard*, *I'm Not Rappaport* and a community play tour of the west country. Since leaving the Old Vic she has designed *The Steamie* and *Don Giovanni* (Greenwich); *The Masterbuilder* and *The Man Who Had All The Luck* (Bristol Old Vic); *Stars in the Morning Sky* (Orange Tree), *Ghosts*, *Second from Last in the Sack Race* and *Who's Afraid of Virginia Woolf* (West Yorkshire Playhouse); *Moll Flanders* (Lyric Hammersmith) and *The Risen People* (Gaiety Theatre, Dublin). She is a senior designer at Imagination Ltd.

JUDITH CROFT

Judith Croft trained at the Bristol Old Vic Theatre School after taking a degree in fashion and textile design. She became resident designer at the Chester Gateway Theatre, then Head of Design at the Coliseum Theatre in Oldham. She freelanced from 1986 until joining the Library Theatre Company, Manchester in 1991 as Head of Design.

Since joining the Company Judith has designed the three shows in Neil Simon's *Brighton Beach Trilogy*, Arthur Miller's *Two Way Mirror*, Ibsen's *Ghosts* and a range of other plays. She has designed work for children including *Peter Pan*, *Jungle Book*, *The Lion, the Witch and the Wardrobe*, and most recently *Alice*, which was produced as a promenade performance in Heaton Park. In October 1993 she designed *Assassins*, the latest musical by Stephen Sondheim, produced by the Library Theatre Company.

BOB CROWLEY

Bob Crowley is one of Britain's leading designers, working in theatre, opera and film. He is an Associate Artist of both the Royal Shakespeare Company and the Royal National Theatre.

Designs for the RSC have included *The Irish Play*, *Thirteenth Night*, *The Forest*, *The Taming of the Shrew*, *King Lear*, *Measure for Measure*, *The Time of Your Life*, *A New Way to Pay Old Debts*, *Henry V*, *Love's Labours Lost*, *As You Like It*, *Les Liaisons Dangereuses* (also West End, New York, Los Angeles and Tokyo), *The Two Noble Kinsmen*, *Flight*, *Principia Scriptorae*, *Macbeth*, *The Jew of Malta*, *The Plantagenets*, *Henry IV Parts I & II*, and tours of *Romeo and Juliet*, *A Midsummer Night's Dream*, *The Winter's Tale*, *The Crucible*, *Othello* and *Hamlet*.

At the Royal National Theatre he has designed *A Midsummer Night's Dream*, *Ghetto*, *Hedda Gabler*, *Ma Rainey's Black Bottom*, *Racing Demon*, *White Chameleon*, *Richard III*, *Murmuring Judges*, *The Sea*, *Night of the Iguana*, *Carousel* (West End and Broadway),

Macbeth and *Absence of War*.

Other work has included *Timon of Athens*, *A View From The Bridge* and *Destiny* (Bristol Old Vic); *A Midsummer Night's Dream* (Bristol Old Vic and London); *The Duchess of Malfi* (Royal Exchange, Roundhouse and Paris); *Dr Faustus* (Royal Exchange); *One of Us* (Greenwich Theatre); *After Aida* (Welsh National Opera and The Old Vic); *Two Way Mirror* (The Young Vic); *Saint Oscar* (Field Day Theatre Company); Mishima's *Madame de Sade* (Tokyo); *The Three Sisters* (Gate Theatre, Dublin and Royal Court, London); *When She Danced* (Globe); *No Man's Land* (Almeida and Comedy), *The Importance of Being Earnest* (Aldwych); *Moonlight* (Almeida and West End); *The Cryptogram* (Ambassadors) and *Hapgood* (Lincoln Center Theater, New York).

Opera designs have included *Don Giovanni* (Kent Opera); *Alcina* (Spitalfields Festival and Los Angeles); *The King Goes Forth To France*, *The Knot Garden*, *La Traviata* and *Anastasia* (Royal Opera House), *The Magic Flute* (English National Opera), *Eugene Onegin* (Welsh National Opera, Opera North and Lyric Opera of Queensland); *Don Giovanni* (Bavarian State Opera) and *The Cunning Little Vixen* (Chatelet, Paris). Designs for film include *Othello*, *Tales of Hollywood* and *Suddenly Last Summer* (BBC). He has also designed for Sting and Duran Duran. He made his directing debut with *The Cure at Troy* for Field Day Theatre Company.

Bob Crowley has received 11 Olivier nominations, two Drama Desk Award nominations (New York) and two Tony Award nominations. In 1990 he won the Olivier Award for Designer of the Year and won the 1994 Tony Award and Outer Critics Circle Award for his work on *Carousel*. He has twice been a member of the British team at the Prague Quadrennial International Stage Design Competition.

ANN CURTIS

Ann Curtis' costume credits include *The Wars of the Roses* (1963), *The Histories Cycle* (1964), *Indians* and *Macbeth* (all in collaboration with John Bury); *The Government Inspector*, *The Romans*, *When Thou Art King* (set and costumes), *Julius Caesar*, *The Devils* (all for the Royal Shakespeare Company); *Moses und Aron*, *The Magic Flute*, *Troilus and Cressida* (Royal Opera House); *Don Carlos*, *A Night in Venice* (English National Opera); *Tom Jones* (English Music Theatre); *A Midsummer Night's Dream* (Royal Opera, Copenhagen); *The Merchant*, *St Joan*, *The Beggar's Opera* (Birmingham Repertory Theatre); *Me and My Girl* (Haymarket Theatre, Leicester, London, New York and touring) and *Tosca* (Opera North). Television and film credits include *Anthony and Cleopatra*, *Man and Superman* and *A Midsummer Night's Dream*.

Her work in Canada has included *Twelfth Night*, *Love for Love*, *King John* and *Othello* for Stratford Festival; *Timon of Athens*, *The Club* (Grand Theatre, London, Ontario); *The Crucible*, *La Bête*, *Cyrano de Bergerac* (Citadel, Edmonton); *Albert Herring*, *The Marriage of Figaro* (Canadian Opera Company, Toronto); *Aspects of Love* (Toronto and US Tour); and the film *The Wars*. Ann Curtis is a Lecturer in the history of costume at Central St Martin's School of Art and Design, London and Visiting Tutor at the National Theatre School of Canada, Montreal.

CHARLES CUSICK SMITH

Charles Cusick Smith graduated in 1978 from Glasgow School of Art and gained a Higher Diploma in Fine Art at the Slade in 1981. He was Arts Council Trainee Designer 1981-82 and has since worked as a designer for drama, musicals and pantomime in regional repertory theatre. His most recent productions are *Plough and the Stars*, *Pacific Overtures* and *Follies* (at the Leicester Haymarket); Tchaikovsky's opera, *The Maid of Orleans* (Royal Northern College of Music, Manchester) and *Giselle* (English National Ballet).

He received the award of Best Designer 1986 from the Manchester Evening News, and the TMA Regional Theatre Award for Best Design for *The Plough and the Stars* in 1993.

PAUL DART

For the Cambridge Theatre Company Paul Dart has designed *The Country Wife*, *Lady Windermere's Fan*, *The Revenger's Tragedy*, *The Game of Love and Chance*, *The Dearly Beloved*, *Les Enfants du Paradis*, *A Handful of Dust*, and *Emma*. Theatre work elsewhere includes *The Cherry Orchard*, *The Wandering Jew*, *Countrymania* (Royal National Theatre); *One Thousand and One Nights* (Bergen); *Marriage* (Heidelberg); *Beauty and the Beast*, *Saturday, Sunday, Monday*, and *When We Are Married* (Birmingham Rep).

In opera he has designed *La Finta Giardiniera* (Lausanne and Frankfurt Opera); *Ariadne auf Naxos* (Lausanne); *Children's Crusade* (Aldeburgh); and in dance *Rite Electric*, *Dance Like Thunder* (London Contemporary Dance Theatre).

He is Head of Design for Obsessions, a chain of gift shops, and Head of Design and Director of James Glancey Designs, responsible for large-scale Christmas and promotional displays.

PETER J DAVISON

Peter J Davison worked at the Royal Opera House from 1977 to 1986 as a design assistant. As an associate designer he has worked with the Brother's Quay on *The Love for Three Oranges* (Opera North and English National Opera), *A Flea in Her Ear* (Old Vic), and *Mazeppa* (Bregenz Festspiele and De Nederlandse Opera).

He has designed many operas including *Mitridate*, *Re di Ponto* (Wexford Festival and the Queen Elizabeth Hall); *Peter Grimes* (Dublin Grand Opera); *L'Ajo nell Imbarazzo* (Battignano); and sets only for *Tosca* (Hong Kong Arts Festival); *Le Nozze de Figaro* (Vienna Festival) and a subsequent new production of *Le Nozze de Figaro* (55 Maggio Musicale, Fiorentino); *Falstaff* (English Touring Opera) and *Falstaff* again (Opernhaus, Zurich); *Die Gezeichneten* (Opernhaus Zurich); *Capriccio* (Deutsche Staatsoper Berlin); *Lucia di Lammermoor* (Welsh National Opera) and *Der Rosenkavalier* (English National Opera and Los Angeles Opera).

His theatre work includes sets for various productions for the Almeida Theatre: *When We Dead Awaken*, *All for Love*, *The Rules of the Game*, *School for Wives* (set and costumes) and *Medea* (transferring to Wyndham's Theatre and subsequently to the Longacre Theatre, Broadway, to critical acclaim). Other works for the theatre have included *Bed* and *The Beaux Stratagem* (Royal National Theatre); *The Liar* (Old Vic); *St Joan* (The Strand) and most recently *Le Cid* (in repertoire at the Cottesloe, Royal National Theatre).

He designed *Strange Fish* (DV8 Physical Theatre) for which he won the Time Out Award 1992. Peter was nominated for a Tony Award, an Olivier Award and a Drama Desk Award for *Medea*.

CECELIA DOIDGE

Cecelia Doidge trained at Guildford and Wimbledon Schools of Art before being awarded a scholarship and Arts Council Bursary to study at Die Höchschule für Bildende Künste in West Berlin. She has designed extensively for theatre, ballet and dance, as well as for film and television companies in England and abroad. Recent design work has been for Ulster Youth Dance and London Contemporary Dance Trust.

HUGH DURRANT

Hugh Durrant studied for an MA in Fine Arts at Magdalene College, Cambridge. He has designed for all sorts of spaces, including fringe venues, thrust stages, the Open Air Theatre in Regent's Park (14 productions) and a cathedral. Work includes many classic and modern productions, pantomimes and musicals, at theatres in Chichester, Bristol, Birmingham and Richmond and with repertory companies at Nottingham, York, Exeter and Birmingham.

He has designed *Babes in the Wood*, *Cinderella*, *The Hot Shoe Show* (all at the Palladium); *Seven Brides for Seven Brothers*, *The Mikado* and *Copacabana* also in the West End; national tours of Britain with *Amadeus*, *A Little Night Music*, *Company*; European premieres of *Mack and Mabel* and *Lady in the Dark*. In dance, he has worked for the Royal Ballet, Dutch National Ballet, Nederlands Dans Theatre, Rambert and La Scala Milan. He has also directed, adapted and written for the stage, designed for television and commercials and designed for fashion (both ready-to-wear and couture) in this country and abroad.

NETTIE EDWARDS

Nettie Edwards trained in Washington and Massachusetts before returning to Britain where she gained an honours degree in theatre design at what was then Trent Polytechnic. She has since worked in repertory theatre around the country including productions of *Three Sisters* (Liverpool Everyman); *Lucky Chance* (York Theatre Royal); *Torch Song Trilogy* (Chester Gateway) and educational tours of *Henry V* and *The Tempest* (Royal National Theatre). She has also worked in television where she was assistant costume designer on *By the Sword Divided*.

As Head of Design at the Duke's Theatre Lancaster, she designed *Nice Loud Voice*, *Sleeping Beauty*, *The Winter's Tale*, *Jude the Obscure*, *The Play of Jennet* and *The Changeling*. She then became Associate Designer at Contact Theatre, Manchester, where she designed *Raisin in the Sun*, *Blood Wedding* (which won Best Design in the Manchester Evening News Theatre Awards), *Dreams with Teeth*, *Antony and Cleopatra*, *The Power of Darkness* and *Playboy of the West Indies*.

She has been Head of Design at the Everyman Theatre, Cheltenham since 1989. Here she has designed productions of *Jungle Book*, *Blue Remembered Hills*, *Death and the Maiden*, *Les Liaisons Dangereuses*, *Annie*, *The Sound of Music*, *Jane Eyre*, *Amadeus*, *All My Sons*, *Macbeth*, *A Doll's House*, *The Cherry Orchard*, *The Pickwick Papers*, *A Family Affair*, *Peter Pan*, *Design for Living*, *Deathtrap*, *The Mayor of Casterbridge*, *A Little Hotel on the Side*, *The Provok'd Wife*, *A View from the Bridge*, *Gaslight* and *The Importance of Being Earnest*. She has also designed *Lady Macbeth* in the Richardson Studio.

ANOUK EMANUEL

Anouk Emanuel graduated from Bristol University in 1988 before training in theatre design at the Central School of Speech and Drama. In 1990 she set up Immediate Design, a design consultancy specialising in theatre and media design and from 1991 until 1994 was also Technical Manager at The Man in the Moon Theatre.

Theatre design work includes *Fings Aint Wot They Used T'Be*, *The Wake of Jamey Foster*, *Tim Pan Ali*, *Dracula* and *Man of Mode* for Arts Educational Schools (Arts Educational and Tabard Theatres); *Ginger* for Spiral (Nuffield Theatre and touring); *Love in the Country* for Actor's Co-operative (Almeida Theatre and The Duke of York's Theatre); *The Boys in the Band* (Man in the Moon Theatre); *Kindertransport*, co-designed with Tom Piper for Soho Theatre Company (Cockpit Theatre); *Othello* (Central School of Speech and Drama); *Approaching Zanzibar*, *The False Count* and *Keeley's Mother* for The Women in the Moon Season (Man in the Moon Theatre); *Cockpit Circus* for Alternative Arts (Cockpit Theatre); *A Yorkshire Tragedy* and *Insignificance* for the RSC (Cockpit Theatre and Young Vic); *Girls Who Wear Glasses* (The King's Head); *Momo and The Time Thieves* for Bristol Reunions (Theatre West End, Edinburgh); *Dr Faustus*, *Inside Stories* and *Trotsky and Our Ernie* (as Resident Designer, Cockpit Theatre 1990-91). For television, she has designed *Fragments* for Shirk Productions. She is currently working for Operascope (Queen Elizabeth Hall, South Bank Centre).

LIS EVANS

Lis Evans trained at Cardiff Art College and then in theatre design at what was Trent Polytechnic. Her first design was for a touring production of *The Wind in the Willows* for Rose Bruford College. From there she then went on to design Circus Senso's acrobatic Christmas show at the Hackney Empire, both directed by John Turner. For the Midland Group, Nottingham, she co-designed costumes and masks for Incompany Theatre's production of *Equus*, which went on to the 1988 Edinburgh Fringe Festival.

After various painting and prop-making contracts for trade and fashion shows and fringe companies, she joined the production department at the New Victoria Theatre, North Staffordshire as Resident Designer. She has designed sets and costumes for over 20 main house shows including *Julius Caesar*, *Sweeney Todd*, *The Hunchback of Notre Dame*, *Twelfth Night*, *A Midsummer Night's Dream*, *The Cherry Orchard* and *The Jolly Potters*. The opportunities presented by theatre in the round continue to present new and exciting design possibilities.

PAUL FARNSWORTH

Paul Farnsworth trained in theatre design at Wimbledon School of Art. He was Resident Designer for a season at Chichester Festival Theatre's new Minerva Studio, designing *Summerfolk*, *Warrior*, *War and Peace* and *Love's Labours Lost*. Other designs have included *A Midsummer Night's Dream*, *The Fire Raisers*, *The Spershott Version*, *Translations*, *Tissue* (Chichester Festival Theatre Tent); *The Pied Piper of Hamelin*, *The Wind in the Willows* (Chichester Festival Theatre); *Huis Clos* (Lyric Theatre, Hammersmith); *Spoils of War* (Leeds Playhouse); *The Cherry Orchard* (Aldwych Theatre); *Peter Pan* (Theatre Clwyd); *Same Old Moon*, *Little Foxes*, *Rough Crossing*, *The Taming of the Shrew*, *On the Razzle* and *Keyboard Skills* (Nuffield Theatre, Southampton); *The Power and the Glory* and *70 Girls 70* (Chichester Festival Theatre and in the West End); *The Fantasticks* (Open Air Theatre, Regent's Park); *The Taming of the Shrew*, *Salt of the Earth*, *Teechers*, *Hedda Gabler* and *The Rocky Horror Show* (Leicester Haymarket Theatre); *Volpone* and *The Merchant of Venice* (English Shakespeare Company); *Good Morning Bill* (Watermill Theatre); the Leslie Bricusse/Anthony Newley musical *Scrooge* (national tour and Australia); the West End production of *Valentine's Day*, and *What a Performance* (Theatre Royal, Plymouth and West End).

Other projects have included *My Father's House* (Birmingham Rep); *Point Valaine, Valentine's Day* and *Adam Was a Gardener* (Chichester Festival Theatre); *Safe Sex* (Contact Theatre, Manchester); *Lady Be Good, A Midsummer Night's Dream* and *A Connecticut Yankee* (Open Air Theatre, Regent's Park); *Moby Dick – A Whale of a Tale* (Piccadilly) and *The Card* (Watermill Theatre). Current work includes *Calamity Jane* at the Leicester Haymarket.

JONATHAN FENSOM

Jonathan Fensom trained in theatre design at Nottingham. His designs for the theatre have included *The Importance of Being Earnest, Billy Liar* and *Wait Until Dark* (Salisbury Playhouse); *September Tide*, (Kings Head and then in the West End); *Cinderella* and *Stevie* (Duke's Playhouse, Lancaster); *The Little Match Girl* (Orange Tree, Richmond); *Yosopov* (Old Fire Station, Oxford and at the Sydmonton Festival); *Lady Macbeth* (Finborough Arms); *Echo Lady* (Theatre Clwyd); he was also co-designer for *Hunting of the Snark* (Leicester Haymarket Studio).

He assisted on the designs for *Five Guys Named Moe* (Stratford East) and *Iron Man* (Young Vic), as well as spending two years assisting Ultz working on *The Thebans* (Royal Shakespeare Company), *Dragon* and *The Resistible Rise of Arturo Ui* (Royal National Theatre).

RICK FISHER

Rick Fisher has worked in British theatre for over 15 years. His lighting designs for *Machinal* at the Royal National Theatre, *Hysteria* at the Royal Court and *Moonlight* at the Almeida and Comedy Theatres won him the 1994 Laurence Olivier Award for Best Lighting Designer. His design for *An Inspector Calls* on Broadway won him the 1994 Tony and Drama Desk Awards and also an Olivier nomination for the London production in 1992.

He has lit numerous shows for the Royal Shakespeare Company including *Misha's Party, All's Well That Ends Well, Artists and Admirers, 'Tis Pity She's A Whore, The Virtuoso, The Alchemist, Two Shakespearean Actors, Restoration, Temptation, Gift of the Gorgon* (also at Wyndham's) and *Some Americans Abroad* (also at the Lincoln Center, New York). At the Royal National Theatre he has designed *Peer Gynt, Black Snow, The Coup, Machinal* and *An Inspector Calls*. He has also designed for the Royal Court and many of London's fringe companies.

For dance he has lit a number of pieces for The Kosh and Adventures in Motion Pictures. Opera work includes *L'Etoile, La Bohème, Peter Grimes* and *Gloriana* (Opera North) and three seasons of outdoor opera for Musica nel Chiostro in Batignano, Italy.

TIM FOSTER ARCHITECTS

Tim Foster Architects is a medium-scale architectural practice which specialises in the design and construction of auditoria and other buildings for the arts. It works with leading consultants in the fields of arts management consultancy, theatre consultancy, acoustic design, mechanical and electrical services design, structural engineering and quantity surveying, co-ordinating their services to suit the needs of particular clients. Successful auditoria must enhance the unique qualities of a live performance, enabling the audiences to relate closely to the performers and amongst themselves. A carefully designed acoustic environment is essential and the complex technical requirements of stage machinery, production lighting, sound systems and ventilation systems must be fully integrated with the architecture.

Major theatre projects carried out by the practice include The Tricycle Theatre (1980 and 1989), The Gate Theatre (1993), The Cliffs Pavilion in Southend-on-Sea (1992) and school theatres at Dulwich College (1981) and St Paul's Boys School (1987).

Tim Foster trained at the Cambridge University School of Architecture where he also designed settings for many stage productions in Cambridge, Edinburgh and London. Before establishing his own practice in 1977, he worked with Roderick Ham and Partners and as consultant architect to Theatre Projects Consultants and was responsible for the design of auditoria for several major performing arts projects world-wide. He is deputy chairman of the ABTT Theatre Planning Committee.

RICHARD FOXTON

Richard Foxton studied theatre design at Trent Polytechnic, graduating in 1989. He is now Resident Designer at the Octagon Theatre, Bolton, where he has designed *The Glass Menagerie* (set only), *Derby Day, Blood Wedding, My Mother Said I Never Should..., A Christmas Carol, Billy Liar* and in the Bill Naughton Theatre, *The Fastest Clock in the Universe* (set only) and *Brimstone and Treacle*. He is currently designing *Mowgli's Jungle* for the Octagon Theatre.

For four years prior to joining the Octagon, he was Assistant/Deputy Resident Designer at Contact Theatre in Manchester where he designed *Man = Man, Excess XS, Woza Albert, The Weirdstone of Brisingamen* (co-designed with Eve Stewart) and *Oedipus Tyrannos* (winner of the 1992 Manchester Evening News Design Award and nominated for the 1992 TMA Regional Theatres Design Award).

Other design work includes *A Clockwork Orange* (TAG, Glasgow); Berkoff's *Kvetch* (West Yorkshire Playhouse), which was nominated for the 1992 TMA Regional Theatres Design Award; *Murderer Hope of Womankind* (International Festival of Expressionism 1992); *Game Challenge Level Seven* (The Hulme, Moss Side and Rusholme Community Play); *God's Grace* (Contact Community Team) and *Ubu*, co-designed with Kevin Pollard (Contact Youth Theatre).

BRUCE GALLUP

Bruce Gallup trained at Wimbledon School of Art and was a finalist in the 1991 Linbury Prize for stage design. Theatre design work includes *Carmen* and *La Bohème* (Beaufort Opera); *Happy Days* (Salberg Studio, Salisbury); *Absurd Person Singular, Same Time Next Year, Bedside Manners, I Ought to be in Pictures, Love en Suite* and *Corpse!* (The Mill at Sonning); *Master Olof* (Christchurch, Spitalfields); *The Cenci* and *Katerina* (Lyric Studio, Hammersmith); *Blues in the Night* and *Leader of the Pack* (Duke of York's, London) and *Lipstick Dreams* (Shaw Theatre and tour).

JANEY GARDINER

Janey Gardiner trained in theatre design at Central St Martin's School of Art and Design where she now teaches history of costume, part time.

As a freelance designer she has designed *Cloud Nine* (Contact Theatre, Manchester) and costumes for *Fashion* (Library Theatre, Manchester). London-based work includes *Pinocchio* and *Beef No Chicken* (Shaw Theatre); *Rainbow Uprising*, a Reggae musical (Lilian Baylis Theatre); *Ghetto* (Riverside Studios). As Associate Designer at the Redgrave Theatre Farnham, 1991-93, productions included *The Kingfisher, Ding Dong Dead, Comedy of Errors, Happy Family* and a commercial tour of *Don't Rock The Boat*. Recent touring work includes *Bitter and Twisted* (Black Theatre Co-op); and *Hereward The Wake* (Eastern Angles).

She is also Visiting Lecturer in costume and design at Northbrook College, Central School of Speech and Drama, Guildford School of Acting and Mountview Theatre School.

MICHAEL E HALL

Michael E Hall became involved in theatre whilst studying engineering at university. He then worked as an electrician for the Glasgow Citizens' and Half Moon Theatres and lighting at York Theatre Royal, where his designs included *Kiss of the Spiderwoman, It's a Girl* and *Romeo and Juliet*.

In Lancaster he has lit two outdoor park seasons and also shows at the Duke's Playhouse including *'Tis Pity She's a Whore* and *Bring Down The Sun*. For the Library Theatre in Manchester his lighting designs include *Brother Eichmann, Robin Hood* and *Two Way Mirror*. He also designed the lighting for *Hamlet* (KAOS Theatre Company); *Andromache* (Camden Studio); *My Cousin Rachel* (Derby Playhouse) and *La Bohème* (English Touring Opera). For the Cheltenham Everyman Michael has provided lighting for *The Mayor of Casterbridge, The Pickwick Papers, Lady Macbeth, Macbeth, Amadeus, My Cousin Rachel, The Sound of Music, The Railway Children, Death and the Maiden, Blue Remembered Hills, And A Nightingale Sang* and *Jungle Book*.

PETER RUTHVEN HALL

Peter Ruthven Hall trained as an architect. He now works as a designer for the leading international design group, Imagination and as a stage designer in the theatre for operas, musicals and plays.

Theatre work includes designs for *The Grapes of Wrath* (Crucible, Sheffield); *Women of Troy, Vassa Zheleznova* (Gate Theatre, London) and *The House of Bernarda Alba* (Oxford Playhouse). In musical theatre, Andrew Lloyd Webber's *Sunset Boulevard* (Sydmonton Festival), *Tutankhamun* (Imagination) and *Merrily We Roll Along* (English Touring Company); and in opera, designs for *Lakmé* (Opera Ireland), *Cosi Fan Tutte, Il Matrimonio Segreto* (Royal Academy of Music), the British premieres of Schubert's *Fierrabras* and *Camacho's Wedding* by Mendelssohn (Oxford Playhouse), and costume designs for *The Turn of the Screw* (Opera Northern Ireland and Royal Northern College of Music), *Zar und Zimmermann* (Aachen Opera), *Don Giovanni* and *Die Zauberflöte* (Vienna Kammeroper). For Imagination, work has included the sets for *Joy to the World* at the Royal Albert Hall from 1989 - 1992, also broadcast on BBC1.

He is currently Honorary Secretary of the Society of British Theatre Designers and administrator for Theatre Design Umbrella.

KEN HARRISON

Ken Harrison trained at the Motley Theatre Design Course 1981-82 and in 1984 was awarded an Arts Council Bursary to work at the Palace Theatre, Watford. He was Associate Designer at Pitlochry Festival Theatre 1989-92 and Head of Design at the Mercury Theatre, Colchester.

Other work has included *Artists and Admirers* (Riverside Studios); *Castles in the Air* (Lyric Theatre, Belfast); *Famine* (Druid Theatre, Galway); *Mirandolina* (Bristol Old Vic Studio); *The American Clock* (York Theatre Royal and Tyne Theatre, Newcastle); *The Red Chair* (Unicorn Theatre for Children); *Hayfever* (New Vic, Stoke-on-Trent); and *Sleeping Beauty* (King's Theatre, Edinburgh).

TIM HATLEY

Tim Hatley trained at the Central School of Art and Design. He won the Dance Commission in the 1989 Linbury Prize for Stage Design, the 1991 Plays and Players Critics Best Designer Award and the 1992 Time Out Award for Best Design.

His work has included *The Misunderstanding* and *Damned For Despair* (Gate Theatre, Notting Hill); *The Taming of the Shrew* and *Hiawatha* (Sheffield Crucible); *Roughcut* (Rambert Dance Company); *Light in the Village, Moscow Stations* and *Poor Super Man* (Traverse Theatre, Edinburgh); *Richard III* (Royal Shakespeare Company); *Chatsky* (Almeida); *Cinderella* (Northern Ballet Theatre); *The Lady from the Sea* (WYP/Lyric Hammersmith); *Orpheus in the Underworld* (Opera North); *Il Trovatore* (Scottish Opera); *Die Fledermaus* and *HMS Pinafore* (D'Oyly Carte Opera) and *The Three Lives of Lucie Cabrol* (Theatre de Complicité).

MARJOKE HENRICHS

Marjoke Henrichs was born in Holland and trained at the Jan van Eyck Academy in Maastricht, and with Margaret Harris in London. She won an Arts Council Bursary in 1988 which resulted in her working for a season at the Royal Lyceum in Edinburgh.

She was Associate Designer at the Wolsey Theatre in Ipswich from 1991-93. Designs include *Romeo and Juliet* (Duke's Playhouse, Lancaster); *The Madman of the Balconies* (Gate, Notting Hill); *A Doll's House, View From the Bridge, Candida, Absent Friends, Dangerous Corner, The Nose, Once in a While The Odd Thing Happens, Key For Two* and *See How They Run* (Wolsey Theatre, Ipswich); *A Family Affair* and *The House of Bernarda Alba* (Royal Lyceum, Edinburgh); *The Importance of Being Earnest* (Century Theatre, Crewe); *Long To Rain Over Us* (Leicester Haymarket); *De Troefkaart* and *Arcadia* (Haarlems Toneel). She is also working on the production design for a short film.

VINCE HERBERT

Vince Herbert trained at LAMDA, but left the course prematurely to teach at the college. Subsequently his career has taken him to the New Shakespeare Company, Theatre Projects Consultants and the Redgrave Theatre.

His work in opera lighting design has taken him to, among other places, the Vienna Festival, Manchester Cathedral and Glasgow, to work with Scottish Opera. Some of his recent national tours have included *Amongst Barbarians, She Stoops to Conquer, Pride and Prejudice, The Miser* and the opera *Cinderella*. Recent theatre productions include *Mother Tongue* (Greenwich); *Macbeth* (Waterside Theatre, Stratford upon Avon) and *Blithe Spirit, The Moonstone, The Brothers Karamazov, Maybe* and *The Count of Monte Cristo*, all at the Royal Exchange Theatre, Manchester.

SIMON HIGLETT

Simon Higlett trained at the Wimbledon School of Art and at the Slade, where he won the Leslie Hurry Prize in 1982. He has designed for theatres in Britain and abroad.

Design credits include: *The Miser* with Tom Courtenay and *The Brothers Karamazov* (Royal Exchange, Manchester); *Scenes from a Marriage* (Chichester and Wyndham's Theatre); *Medea* (Young Vic); *Winnie* (Victoria Palace);

Antony and Cleopatra; *The Taming of the Shrew*; *Singer* (Royal Shakespeare Company at the Barbican); *Kean* (Old Vic); *The Cabinet Minister* (Albery Theatre); *The Mother Tongue* and *Broadway Bound* (Greenwich); *Making it Better* (Criterion Theatre); *Rope* and *The Lion in Winter* (national tour); *The Crucible* (Sheffield Crucible); Alan Bennett's *Talking Heads* (national tour and Comedy Theatre); *King Lear in New York, Double Take, The Sisterhood, Ricochet, A Doll's House, Dangerous Corner* and *The Three Sisters* (Chichester Festival Theatre).

He has been Head of Design for the New Shakespeare Company in Regent's Park, during which time he re-designed the stage area. Opera design credits include *Seraglio* (Scottish Opera); *La Cenerentola* (Vienna, Brighton and London opera festivals); *Cosi Fan Tutte, Don Giovanni* and *The Marriage of Figaro* (Music Theatre London and Hamburg) and more recently, *La Traviata* (Covent Garden Opera Festival) and *The Barber of Seville* (Germany).

PAMELA HOWARD

Pamela Howard trained at Birmingham College of Art and the Slade School of Fine Art in London. Her theatre work includes designs for Birmingham Repertory Theatre, Nottingham Playhouse, Chichester Festival Theatre, Tramway, Glasgow and the Royal National Theatre. She designed *Border Warfare* and *John Brown's Body* for John McGrath at the Tramway. *John Brown's Body* was part of the British exhibit at the Prague Quadrennial International Exhibition in 1991 which won the Golden Triga award for Best National Exhibit. She has been associated for many years with work at Theatre National Populaire in Villeurbane, France.

Recently she has designed *The Revenger's Tragedy, Three Girls in Blue, Wicked Old Man, Happy Days* (West Yorkshire Playhouse); *The Madras House* (Lyric, Hammersmith and Edinburgh Festival 1992 – Edinburgh Critic's Award); *The Plough and the Stars* (O'Casey Theatre Company, USA and tour of Ireland), *Behind the Green Curtains* (O'Casey Theatre Company, USA) and *Macbeth* (Theatre Clwyd). Productions with the Royal Shakespeare Company include *Othello, The Taming of the Shrew* and *Elgar's Rondo*; with the Royal National Theatre: *Yerma, School for Wives, The Philanderer* (costumes) and *Sergeant Musgrave's Dance* (costumes); and for television *Border Warfare, John Brown's Body* and *Suffer Little Children* (BBC2).

Pamela Howard teaches at Birmingham and Croydon Art Schools and has also been Director of Theatre Design at Central Saint Martin's College of Art and Design, London. She is now founder and director of the European Scenography Centres, an International Masters Course in Theatre Design in London, Prague, Barcelona and Utrecht.

She has been Advisory Editor to *British Theatre Design: The Modern Age* (Weidenfeld and Nicholson, 1989). A current commission is *Scenography*, part of the *Theatre in Context* series to be published in 1995. She has also published articles in *New Theatre Quarterly, Sightlines, and Theatre Design and Technology* (USA).

A former Honorary Secretary of the Society of British Theatre Designers and currently the international co-ordinator for Great Britain for the 1995 Prague Quadrennial, she is also a member of the International Organisation for Theatre Designers.

As a director her work includes *La Celestina* (workshop production, Almeida Theatre) and *Shakespeare's Universe* (Barbican Arts Centre).

RICHARD HUDSON

Richard Hudson's extensive work in the theatre includes *Andromache, One Way Pendulum, Bussy D'Ambois, The Tempest, Too Clever by Half, Candide* and *King Lear* (Old Vic); *La Bête* (Eugene O'Neill Theatre, Broadway for which he was nominated for a Tony, and Lyric, Hammersmith); *Into the Woods* (Phoenix Theatre); *The Misanthrope* (Bristol Old Vic and Royal National Theatre); *Travesties* (Royal Shakespeare Company and Savoy Theatre), *The Master Builder* and *A Clockwork Orange* (Royal Shakespeare Company); *Desire and Hippolytos* (Almeida); *The Emperor* (Royal Court); *Bohemian Lights* (Gate Theatre, London); *Don Carlos* (Royal Exchange, Manchester); *Twelfth Night* (Goodman Theatre, Chicago); and *Oklahoma!* currently on a national tour. In 1988 he won the Lawrence Olivier Award for design for his season at the Old Vic.

For opera he has designed *L'Inganno Felice* (Rossini Opera Festival, Pesaro); *Yevgeny Onyegin* and *The Queen of Spades* (Glyndebourne Festival); *Les Contes d'Hoffman* (Vienna Staatsoper); *Die Meistersinger von Nurnberg* (Royal Opera House); *The Force of Destiny* and *Figaro's Wedding* (English National Opera); *Lucia de Lammermoor* (Zurich Opera and Bayerisches Staatsoper, Munich); *A Night at the Chinese Opera* and *Count Ory* (Kent Opera); *Candide, La Vie Parisienne, The Vanishing Bridegroom* and *Mary Stuart* (Scottish Opera); *Don Pasquale* (Opera Northern Ireland); *Manon* (Opera North) and *Mignon* (Wexford).

HUNTLEY MUIR

Su Huntley and Donna Muir have worked together since the early 80s and have produced some of the most striking and influential images of the last decade. Their work has spanned print, video, book jackets, murals, Royal Mail stamps, and paintings for Grosvenor House Hotel and British Airways Terminal 4. They have exhibited in London, New York and Paris, at the RCA, the Thumb Gallery, in three solo exhibitions in Los Angeles, at the Davies Gallery and most recently at the Royal National Theatre. Besides commissioned print work for magazines and publications of every kind throughout Europe, they have designed posters for Channel 4, the Royal Opera House and ENO, among many others; album covers for Sting and Joan Armatrading; pop videos, commercials, animation, and dance for Canadian National Ballet. They have also designed giant murals both in Los Angeles and for a baseball stadium in Japan and have completed their first stage design for the premiere of the opera *Playing Away* staged by Opera North and Bayerische Staatsoper, Munich.

IMAGINATION ENTERTAINMENTS

Imagination Entertainments is led by producers Jeremy Sturt and Kenny Wax. Dedicated to creating spectacular and imaginative new theatrical events, the company is now working with a variety of young producers, writers and directors to break new ground and create real innovation within the entertainment industry. Imagination Entertainments' projects include the current production of *Once On This Island*, now playing at the Island Theatre, London. This offers the audience a complete island experience, within a totally Caribbean environment.

The company is also responsible for concept design on Barry Manilow's new musical *Copacabana* at London's Prince of Wales Theatre, and design coordination of Peter and Jim Sheridan's production of *The Risen People* at The Gaiety Theatre, Dublin. Previous productions include the royal gala performance of *An Evening with Dylan Thomas*, and the premiere of *Tutankhamun*, a new musical which the company is continuing to develop.

ROBERT JONES

Robert Jones graduated from the Central School of Art and Design. He has been Head of Design at Newcastle Playhouse, Nottingham Playhouse and most recently, from 1990 to 1992, at the newly-built West Yorkshire Playhouse where his designs included *Wild Oats, Carousel, The Maple Tree Game, What Every Woman Knows* and *Playboy of the Western World*.

Freelance design credits include *Private Lives, Look Back in Anger* (Bristol Old Vic); *The Secret Rapture* (Drama-Logue Critics Award for best scenic design, Los Angeles); *Colours* (Abbey Theatre, Dublin); *Getting Attention* (Royal Court Theatre); *Bold Girls* and *Back Up The Hearse* (Hampstead Theatre); national tours of *The Hobbit, Salt of the Earth, Happy Families, April in Paris* and *The Office Party*, all directed by John Godber.

In the West End he has designed *Rosencrantz and Guildenstern are Dead* (Piccadilly); *And Then There Were None* (Duke of York's); *The Pope and the Witch* (Comedy Theatre); and *April in Paris (Ambassadors)*.

Recent freelance work also includes *Romeo and Juliet, Dangerous Corner* and *Rope* (Birmingham Rep); *All God's Chillun Got Wings* and *Someone to Watch Over Me* (West Yorkshire Playhouse); *Big Night Out at the Little Sands Picture Palace* (Nottingham Playhouse); *Democracy* (Bush Theatre), and *A Collier's Friday Night* (Hampstead Theatre), both directed by John Dove; *Pentecost* by David Edgar (Royal Shakespeare Company) and *The Prime of Miss Jean Brodie* (Strand Theatre). He was a member of the British entry at the 1987 Prague Quadrennial exhibition of theatre design.

SANJA JURCA

Sanja Jurca was born in Ljubljana, Slovenia and graduated from Ljubljana University Department of Architecture in 1984. During her studies she took an interest in theatre and began to take part as a designer for the theatre productions of The Ljubljana Academy of Dramatic Arts. The title of her diploma thesis was "The Analysis of Relationships between Architectural and Scenic Space of Acting applied to Genet's *The Maids*". After graduation she started working as a freelance designer in professional theatres in Slovenia.

Since 1984 Sanja Jurca has collaborated on numerous productions in all major Slovene theatres both as costume and stage designer. Her work includes modern Slovene and Yugoslav plays as well as world classics such as Shakespeare and Strindberg. In 1987 she was awarded the Zlata Ptica (Golden Bird) National Prize for young artists. In the same year she was offered a scholarship to participate in Ingmar Bergman's Dramaten Theatre in Stockholm.

Sanja Jurca now works from London in private practice with her husband Selçuk Avci. Their practice is involved in theatre design as well as design of exhibitions, arts centres, theatres and art galleries. Since 1988 Sanja has completed ten productions in the UK including *Singer* (RSC), *The Abduction* (Lumiere & Son at the ICA) and most recently the opera *L'Elisir D'Amore* for the Chichester Festival. She is currently working on a new production of Camus's Caligula for Ljubljana Repertory Theatre in Slovenia.

DAVID KNAPMAN

David Knapman originally trained in exhibition and interior design and window display. He began his theatre career at The Swan Theatre, Worcester. 1973 saw the opening of the new Queen's Theatre, Hornchurch where he joined as Assistant Designer later becoming Head of Design during his five-year stay. Whilst at Hornchurch he was responsible for design work on many new plays including five David Wood premieres and the West End transfer of *Tommy*, the rock opera by Pete Townsend and The Who.

He became Head of Design for The Wolsey Theatre, Ipswich for its opening in 1979. Work there includes *The Three Sisters, Shadowlands* and *No Man's Land*. Other work includes fringe at The Arts Theatre, Upstream Theatre, the Bourse Theatre in Brussels and national tours of *Ring Round the Moon, Little Shop of Horrors, Loot* and Barbara Ewing's play *Alexandra Kollontai* (Leicester Haymarket Studio and ICA, London).

Recent work includes *Into the Woods* which received the TMA award for Best Musical; *The Double Dealer*, with Paul Eddington (national tour) and *Shirley Valentine* (The Drum, Plymouth and Gdansk).

RALPH KOLTAI

Ralph Koltai studied at the Central School of Art and Design. His first production was the opera *Angelique* at the Fortune Theatre, London in 1950. He has since designed almost 200 plays, operas, ballets and musicals all over the world.

His recent work has included *Madam Butterfly* directed by David Pountney (Tokyo); *Otello* directed by Michael Bogdanov (Essen, Germany); *My Fair Lady* for Frank Dunlop (tour of USA) and *Cruel Garden* directed by Lindsay Kemp (Deutsche Opera, Berlin).

As Associate Designer of the Royal Shakespeare Company, 1965-87, he designed 25 productions. He has also designed for the National Theatre, the Royal Opera House, the Royal Ballet and English National Opera.

Ralph Koltai has received numerous awards including The London Drama Critics Award in 1967 for *Little Murders, As You Like It* and *The Love Girl and the Innocent*. In 1975 he was the joint winner of the Individual Gold Medal at the Prague Quadrennial International Exhibition of Scenography; in 1978 he was the Society of West End Theatre Designer of the Year (for *Brand*); in 1979 he was joint winner of the Golden Troika National Award in Prague; in 1983 he was made a CBE; in 1984 he was elected to the Royal Society of Arts and was once again SWET Designer of the Year (for *Cyrano de Bergerac*) and in 1994 he was elected Fellow of the Academy of Perfoming Arts in Hong Kong.

PAUL KONDRAS

From devised, politically correct theatre-in-education to Vodka Martinis with Harry Dean Stanton, Paul Kondras has zig-zagged from one job to the next for over 18 years, designing more than 100 productions.

High spots have included *Hostages* by Bernard McClaverty (Granada Television); several plays by Vince Foxhall, including an adaptation of *Slaughterhouse 5* (Liverpool Everyman) *Racing Demon* and *Death and the Maiden* with Chris Honer (Library Theatre, Manchester).

Future plans include designing a

cod-liver oil television commercial, a beer commercial for PSA in downtown Whalley Range, designs for *The Secret Garden* (Library Theatre) and the re-launch of the launch of the Plonski Brothers with the Polish director Gabriel Gawin.

ANTHONY LAMBLE
Anthony Lamble studied Fine Art in Cheltenham before attending the Theatre Design Course in Islington under the direction of Margaret Harris. During that time he designed *Oral Treason* for the Almeida Music Festival at the Queen Elizabeth Hall, later televised for the BBC.

Theatre credits include *Pale Performer*, *Murder in the Rue Morgue*, *The Naked Pericles* and *The Winter's Tale* (Leicester Haymarket); *Looking at You (Revived) Again*, *The Evildoers* (Bush Theatre); *Blue Night in the Heart of the West* (Bush Theatre and Traverse, Edinburgh Festival 1993); *Ice Cream and Hot Fudge* (Contact Theatre, Manchester); *Whale, Solomon and the Big Cat* and *True West* (Sheffield Crucible); *Three Judgements in One* (Gate Theatre); and *Trilby and Svengali* for Shared Experience.

Most recent designs include *King Baby* (RSC, The Pit); *Pond Life* and *Not Far Away* (Bush Theatre); *Trios* (Riverside Studios); *Burning Everest* (West Yorkshire Playhouse) and *Waiting for Godot* (Lyric Hammersmith and Theatre Royal Plymouth). Current productions (1994) include *Wolf* (Traverse Theatre); *Mortal Ash* (Bush Theatre) and *No Man's Land* for English Touring Theatre (Belgrade, Coventry).

BRIAN LEE
Brian Lee is Head of Design for the National Youth Theatre of Great Britain. He began his career in the original London cast of *Jesus Christ Superstar* and his early experience in the music business has been put to considerable use as a designer in his work on *Godspell* (current national tour); *Behold the Man* (Channel 4) and the NYT musical productions of *Nightshriek*, *Maggie May* and *Blitz!* (subsequently recreated for Northern Stage at the Tyne Theatre and Opera House). Other NYT designs include *The Caucasian Chalk Circle*, *Murder in the Cathedral* (also at the Edinburgh Festival and Moscow Arts Theatre); *Blood Wedding*, *Marat/Sade*, *The Tempest Variations* and *The Rivals*. He recently designed *On Approval* (Watermill Theatre, Newbury).

Abroad he designed the tenth anniversary celebrations of the Mozambique National Dance Company; *Romeo and Juliet* and *Macbeth* (Madrid); *The Flying Dutchman*, *Carmina Burana* and *Dances of Fortune* (Valencia's Palau de la Musica); and Lorca's *Bodas de Sangre* (Teatrejove de Espana) which toured Spain and played at the Mainz Festival.

Brian Lee has led the re-vitalisation of the NYT's design departments. In the process many opportunities have been given to young designers, often in collaboration with the Linbury Prize for Stage Design.

MARK LEESE
Mark Leese trained at the Grays School of Art, Aberdeen and at Duncan of Jordanstone, Dundee. Theatre designs include *The Grapes of Wrath* and *Antigone* (7 84); *The Hope Slide* and *Brothers of Thunder* (Traverse Theatre, Edinburgh); *Snow White, Love and Liberty*, and *The Bloody Chamber* (Tron, Glasgow); *The Steamie* (Brunton Theatre); *Romeo and Juliet* and *Don Juan Comes Back from the War* (New Stage Theatre); *The Homosexual* (TV Productions); *Bill's New Frock*, *Alfreda Abbot's Lost Voice* and *Peacemaker* (Visible Fictions); *Somewhere for Clanjamfrie*, *The Fall of Kelvin Walker*, *Tartuffe* and *The Oedipus Trilogy* (Glasgow Arts Centre); *American Buffalo* (Act I).

Mark Leese is Associate Director of TV Productions and has directed and designed many short films and videos.

JANE LINZ ROBERTS
After training as a member of the Cockpit and National Youth Theatres, Jane Linz Roberts trained at the Central School of Art and Design and the Drama Department of Bristol University.

In 1985 she established 'Scene' with lighting designer Nick MacLiammoir. Together they worked in community theatre, youth theatre and theatre-cabaret. Moving to London, Jane concentrated on small-scale touring and new writing, returning several times to companies such as Perspectives, Avon Touring, Derby Playhouse Studio Company and the Women's Theatre Group. Shows include *On the Plastic* by Julie Wilkinson, *Lear's Daughters*, a devised piece, and *A Prick Song for the New Leviathan* by James Stock. She has also worked extensively in theatre-in-education with, amongst others, Sheffield Crucible TIE, Theatre Centre, Nottingham Playhouse and Roundabout. Jane was a co-founder of the Designers Formation, the first agency for designers.

In 1991 she became Resident Designer for the Sherman Theatre in Cardiff working in both main and studio spaces and again in parallel with Nick MacLiammoir. Her work has ranged from classic plays to new writing and was seen throughout Wales and on tour in England and America. She was also invited to work with several other Welsh companies. Recent productions include *Macbeth*, *Of Mice and Men*, *The Snow Queen* and *The Merchant of Venice*. A new area of work was a design for the visitor centre at the Rhondda Heritage Park. She returned to freelance work in 1994.

EDWARD LIPSCOMB
Edward Lipscomb graduated from Wimbledon School of Art in 1979, since when he has divided his time equally between working in theatre and television set design. His designs have been seen at the Stephen Joseph Theatre in Scarborough (where he was resident designer for four years), Greenwich Theatre, London Festival Ballet, Newcastle Playhouse and Theatre Royal, Lyric Theatre Belfast, The Warehouse, Croydon and numerous productions for the Perth Theatre. In the London's West End he designed Alan Ayckbourn's productions of *Seasons Greetings* (Lyric) and *Intimate Exchanges* (Ambassadors); and in Houston, Texas with the same author/director *Way Upstream* and *Absent Friends*.

Television work includes *Precious Bane*, *The Temptations of Eileen Hughes*, *One Last Chance*, *A Likely Lad*, *Casualty*, *Growing Pains* and *Eastenders*. He is currently Head of Design at Pitlochry Festival Theatre.

CLAIRE LYTH
Claire Lyth read Drama, History and English at Bristol University. She was Head of Design at Liverpool Playhouse and then Royal Lyceum, Edinburgh.

Theatre designs include Dario Fo's *Archangels Don't Play Pinball* (Bristol Old Vic); *Rigoletto* (tour for Welsh National Opera); *Candida* (Arts Theatre, London); *Streamers* (Roundhouse, London); *Split Second* (Lyric Hammersmith); *Tosca*, *Macbeth*, *The Winter's Tale* (Liverpool Everyman); *Oklahoma!* (National tour); *My Cousin Rachel* and *Deadly Embrace* (Bromley); *Same Time Next Year* (Old Vic, London); *Agnes of God* (Greenwich Theatre); *The Young Apollo* (Thorndike, Leatherhead); *A Tale of Two Cities* (tour) and *The Pilgrim* (tour).

She has worked several times in Hong Kong where designs include *Royal Hunt of the Sun*, *Cosi Fan Tutte* and *Rigoletto*. In Denmark she has designed *My Fair Lady* (Aarhus); *When I Was a Girl I Used to Scream and Shout* and *Fallen Angels* (Copenhagen).

Work in the last two years includes *Peter Pan* and *The Three Musketeers* (Sheffield Crucible); *Chicago* (tour); National Opera Studio Showcase 1993 (Queen Elizabeth Hall); *Macbeth*, *Twelfth Night* and *The Fantastical History of Dr Faustus* (English Shakespeare Company); *Single Spies* (Salisbury Playhouse); *As You Like It* and *Othello* (Ludlow Festival); *Beowulf* (Odense Theater, Denmark). She is currently designing Strindberg's *Gustav III* (Aalborg Theater, Denmark).

NICK MACLIAMMOIR
Nick MacLiammoir read chemistry at Bristol University before becoming a lighting designer. Work with Avon Touring Company and Perspectives led to two years as Resident Lighting Designer at the Albany Empire in London. Shows in this period include *A Prick Song for the New Leviathan* by James Stock and *On the Plastic* by Julie Wilkinson, as well as collaborations with directors Hettie MacDonald, Paulette Randall and Claire Grove.

In 1985 he formed the design partnership Scene with Jane Linz Roberts and in 1991 they moved to Cardiff to become Resident Designers at the Sherman Theatre. Designs there include *Of Mice and Men*, *The Merchant of Venice*, *Under Milk Wood* and *The Dark is Rising*.

Freelance since 1993, his recent work has included *Macbeth*, *The Snow Queen* and *Ghosts* (Sherman Theatre); and shows for Made in Wales, Y Cwmni, Public Parts and Dalier Sylw, collaborating with directors and writers such as Jamie Garven, Sean Matthias, Jane Buckler and Ed Thomas.

He also works with youth and community projects throughout Britain and teaches design for the Royal Opera House.

IAN MacNEIL
Ian MacNeil trained at Croydon School of Art and in America. Theatre work has included seasons at the Library Theatre, Manchester (as an Arts Council trainee) and the Birmingham Rep.

Repertory work has included productions for Derby Playhouse, Cheltenham Everyman and the Duke's Theatre, Lancaster; *The Caucasian Chalk Circle* and *The Idiot* (Contact Theatre, Manchester); *Tally's Blood* (Traverse, Edinburgh); *Pavanne* (The Hollywood) and *Manon Lescaut* (Dublin Grand Opera).

Recent work includes *Figaro Gets Divorced*, *Don Gil of the Green Breeches*, *Pioneers in Ingolstadt* and *Purgatory in Ingolstadt*, *Crackwalker* and *Jerker* (The Gate, Notting Hill); *Talking in Tongues* and *Death and the Maiden* (Royal Court); *Ariodante* (English National Opera); and *Macbeth* (Royal Shakespeare Company).

For the Royal National Theatre he designed *An Inspector Calls*, which won him an Olivier Award for Best Designer in 1993 and a Critics' Circle Award. The production subsequently transferred from the Lyttleton to the Olivier, to the Aldwych, Broadway and Japan. He also designed *Machinal* in the Lyttleton Theatre.

CHRISTINE MARFLEET
Christine Marfleet studied Drama at Bristol University where she spent nearly all her time designing and painting productions. The Glynne Wickham Studio space was extremely versatile and everything she designed was subject to public performance. Her first job was as a design assistant at Royal Holloway College, London University, and then as an assistant at the Newcastle Playhouse. Working with experienced repertory designers, directors and production teams gave her the technical knowledge, confidence and support to design professionally.

She has now worked as resident and freelance designer for 11 years, designing sets and costumes for main house repertory theatres, studios, theatres-in-the-round and outdoor spaces. She has worked extensively with theatre-in-education companies and middle- to small-scale touring companies. She was Design Tutor with the Hope Street Project in Liverpool.

She is currently designing productions with Theatr Powys, touring to many venues throughout Wales.

HANNAH MAYALL
Hannah Mayall trained at Wimbledon School of Art (1987) and designed a season of six plays at the Liverpool Playhouse including *Low Level Panic* and *The Beaux Stratagem*.

As a founder member of Altered States Theatre Company, established to commission and produce new plays, she designed *Fears and Miseries...*, *Legends of Evil*, *Self Catering...* and *Boy*. For the London Bubble she has designed the pantomimes, *Ol' King Cole* and *Cinderella* and two summer seasons including *The Good Person of Sezuan*, *Measure for Measure* and *The Giraffe, the Pelly and Me*. She has also designed productions of Rousseau's *Tale* and Corneille's *Polyeucte* for the Gate Theatre, Notting Hill and Aphra Behn's *Sir Patient Fancy* for the Guildhall.

CLAUDIA MAYER
Claudia Mayer trained on the Theatre Design Course at English National Opera, now the Motley Theatre Design Course.

Her work in the theatre includes *A Midsummer Night's Dream* (Broomhill Trust); *Mongrel's Heart* (Royal Lyceum, Edinburgh); *Os Misterios de Chester* (London Theatre Ensemble); *The Guardsman*, *The Constant Wife*, and *For Queen and Country* (Theatre Clwyd); *Marquis of Keith* (Gate Theatre, Notting Hill); *Judgement Day* (Old Red Lion, Islington); *Pig in a Poke* (Oxford Stage Company); *Last of the Red Hot Lovers* (West Yorkshire Playhouse); costumes for *Coriolanus* (Young Vic, London); *A Whistle in the Dark* (Druid at the Royal Court); *Salonika* (Liverpool Playhouse); *Tea in a China Cup* (Riverside Studios, London). She was Head of Design at the Victoria Theatre, Stoke-on-Trent where designs include *The Beggar's Opera*, *Henry IV parts I and II*, *Oedipus the King*, *Hamlet*, *Cider with Rosie*, and *Aesop's Fables*.

Opera and dance designs include *A Midsummer Night's Dream*, *La Serva Padrona*, *Twin Oaks* (Broomhill Trust); *Echoes*, *The Wheel* (Garden Venture '91 and '93); *Mahagonny Singspiel* (City of Birmingham Symphony Orchestra); *Falstaff* (Pimlico Opera); *Eugene Onegin* (British Youth Opera); *The Merry Widow* (Opera 80); costumes for *Hobson's Choice*, and *Meridian* (Birmingham Royal Ballet).

She has worked with many fringe and touring companies including Monstrous Regiment, Metro Theatre Co, Joint Stock, Common Stock, 7:84 England, Soho Poly and Pip Simmons. She has also worked as costume designer on various films and videos.

TANYA McCALLIN
Tanya McCallin trained at the Central School of Art and Design in London.

After a period designing for several principal repertory companies through out Britain and many fringe companies in London, she joined the Hampstead Theatre. There she designed *Dusa, Fish, Stas* and *Vi* (transferred to the Mayfair Theatre, and Paris); Mike Leigh's *Abigail's Party* (also seen on BBC Television) and *The Elephant Man* (also the National Theatre); James Saunder's *Bodies* (also at the Ambassadors Theatre); *The Hard Shoulder* (also Aldwych); *Sufficient Carbohydrate* (also at the Albery) and *A Little Like Drowning* by Anthony Minghella.

Other credits include *Macbeth, Uncle Vanya, Betrayal* and *Mourning Becomes Electra* (Melbourne Theatre Company, Australia); *Bread, They Are Dying Out, Don Juan Returns from the War* and *Who's Afraid of Virginia Woolf?* (National Theatre, London); *A Nightingale Sang, Before the Party* (transferred to the Apollo) and *Women Beware Women* (all at the Oxford Playhouse); *School for Scandal, The Changeling, Waiting for Godot, The Homecoming* and *The Late Christopher Bean* (Cambridge Theatre Company); *My Mother Said I Never Should* by Charlotte Keatley (Royal Court); *Uncle Vanya*, translated by Michael Frayn (Vaudeville Theatre); *Exchange* (Nuffield Theatre and the Vaudeville); costumes for Arthur Miller's *After The Fall* (National Theatre) and sets and costume for Claire Tomalin's *The Winter Wife* (Nuffield Theatre and Lyric Hammersmith)

More recently she has designed Arthur Miller's new play *The Ride Down Mount Morgan* (Wyndhams Theatre); *Hawks and Doves* (Nuffield); *Obsession* (Battersea Arts Centre); *I'm No Angel* (Nuffield) and *Hamlet* (Open Air Theatre, Regents Park).

Her opera work has included Jonathan Miller's production of *The Barber of Seville* (ENO).

ACE McCARRON
Ace McCarron works regularly for The Wrestling School, Music Theatre Wales, and used to work for the Royal Opera House Garden Venture.

Recent work includes *Smoke* and *Blues for Mr Charlie*, which won the Manchester Evening News design team award (Manchester Royal Exchange); *How to Act Better* for Annie Griffin (Riverside Studios); *Suicide and Manipulation* (Finborough Theatre); *A Taste of Honey* (English Touring Theatre); *Ariadne auf Naxos* for Jonathan Miller (Broomhill Theatre, Kent); *Bohemian Lights* and *Cheating Hearts* (Gate, Notting Hill); *Hated Nightfall* by Howard Barker (Wrestling School); *King Lear* (Talawa Theatre Company); *Falling Over England* (Greenwich Theatre); *The Way of the World, The Madness of George III* and *The Rivals* (York Theatre Royal); *The Lighthouse* (Music Theatre Wales); *The Indian Queen* (Scottish Early Music Consort); *Dancing Girls* (Cinnabar Theatre Company); *Great Expectations* (Oxford Stage Company and Watford Palace Theatre); *Siren Song* (Almeida Music Festival); *Wax* (Paines Plough); *Wolf* (Plain Clothes) and *On the Verge of Exploding* (John Bright Company).

ANTHONY McDONALD
Anthony McDonald has designed almost all of the Second Stride shows since 1982 and has worked extensively for opera, theatre and dance. Apart from his work with Second Stride his designs for opera include *Cherubin* (Royal Opera House); *Francesca da Rimini* (Bregenz); *A Midsummer Night's Dream* (Aix-en-Provence Festival); *Billy Budd* (English National Opera); *Orlando* (Scottish Opera); *The Midsummer Marriage* (Opera North and Scottish Opera); *The Trojans* (Welsh National Opera, Opera North, Scottish Opera and Opera de Nice); *Benvenuto Cellini* (Netherlands Opera) and *The Marriage of Figaro* (Australian Opera Company).

Theatre design work includes *War Crimes, Secret Gardens* and *Princess of Cleves* (ICA, London); *Mrs Gaugin, Venice Preserv'd* and *Hedda Gabler* (Almeida Theatre, London); *A Streetcar Named Desire* (Crucible, Sheffield); *Berenice* (Royal National Theatre); *Mad Forest* (Central School and Royal Court); *Richard II* and *Hamlet* (Royal Shakespeare Company); *The Seagull, Hamlet* and *Black Snow* (American Repertory Theatre).

In 1992 he directed *The Birthday Party* at Glasgow Citizens. He directed and designed *Escape at Sea* for Second Stride in 1993.

Future plans include the designs for a new ballet by Ashley Page for the Royal Ballet, for *Pelléas et Mélisande* at Opera North and a new production of *Nabucco* for Welsh National Opera and the Royal Opera House, Covent Garden.

BRUCE McLEAN
Bruce McLean was born in Glasgow. He trained at Glasgow School of Art and St Martin's. His work has been exhibited in Sydney, Atlanta, Seattle, New York, Tokyo and throughout Europe and is in many collections, including the Tate Gallery, Victoria and Albert Museum, Royal Museum of Scotland, National Gallery of Modern Art, Edinburgh, Glasgow Museum, Royal Museum of Scotland, National Gallery of Modern Art, Edinburgh, Glasgow Museums and Art Galleries, South Bank Centre,London, University of Southampton, Harris Museum and Art Gallery, Preston, Aberdeen Art Gallery, Van Abbemuseum, Eindhoven and major collections in Japan. He has been involved in performance art and has made several short films. He designed Ashley Page's *Soldat* (Rambert Dance Company); *The Empress of Newfoundland* (Channel 4) and *Renard* (The Royal Ballet). He has received many awards including a major one from the Arts Council (1975), DAAD, Berlin (1981), and the John Moores Painting Prize (1985). His commissioned works include *Platform Painting* (1991) at Tottenham Hale Station and *Ludgate Head* (1992) at Ludgate.

IONA McLEISH
Although Iona McLeish has designed for a wide range of dance, drama and opera projects, she is best known for her collaboration with women directors and writers on new work. The most recent example of this is *From the Mississippi Delta* directed by Annie Castledine.

Iona's past collaborations with Annie Castledine have included *My Mother Said I Never Should* (Chichester Festival Theatre) and *The Caretaker* (Sherman Theatre, Cardiff). Other work includes two plays by Timberlake Wertenbaker: *For the Love of a Nightingale* directed by Gary Hynes (Royal Shakespeare Company) and *New Anatomies* directed by Nancy Duiguid (Women's Theatre Group); *Heart of Ice* directed by Hilary Westlake (Lumiere & Son);*Hamlet*, directed by Rob Walker (Half Moon); *Hard Times* directed by Nancy Duiguid (Hampstead Theatre); *Medea* directed by Mary McMurray (Lyric Hammersmith); *Savannah Bay* (Foco Novo) and *Eden Cinema* (Off Stage Theatre), both by Marguerite Duras and directed by Lily Susan Todd; Rodney Ackland's *Old Ladies* directed by Annie Castledine (Greenwich Theatre) and *White Sail Black Sail* by Hélène Cixous (Sphinx at the Gate Theatre, and tour).

Designs for dance have included *New Cities Ancient Lands* and *Configurations* (Shobanah Jeyasing Dance Company). She has also designed musicals, and light entertainment shows for Wayne Sleep.

She received the Time Out London Theatre Award for *Heresies* by Deborah Levy, directed by Lily Susan Todd (Royal Shakespeare Company) and was nominated for the Plays and Players Critics Award for *Savannah Bay*

MADELEINE MILLAR
Madeleine Millar studied Theatre Design at Trent Polytechnic. Some time later she began to make sculpture out of welded scrap metal, and to develop her particular theatre design style.

Her favourite work has been multi-locational, multi-levelled, simple, abstract, sculptural sets, drawings through space with thin metal line against soft fabric and drapery, sets that can be climbed into, under, over and that can be played like a musical instrument. She enjpys designing intricate and fantastical costumes where she can play with detail and texture.

She has worked with Leeds Playhouse Theatre-in-Education, Red Ladder, Pit Prop, Public Parts, Theatr Powys, West Yorkshire Playhouse and with directors such as Julia Limer, Carola Luther, John Haslet, Gail McIntyre, and Louise Osborn. She is now studying for an MA in Art and Design to develop even further the relationship between her sculptural work and theatre design.

TIM MITCHELL
Tim Mitchell has lit over 60 productions throughout the UK and the continent. During a long association with the Birmingham Repertory Theatre he has lit *The Playboy of the Western World, Awake and Sing, The Atheist's Tragedy, Old Times, Romeo and Juliet, Rope, Big Maggie, The Wizard of Oz, Nervous Women, The Grapes of Wrath, All My Sons, The Ragged Trousered Philanthropist* (national tour), *Cider with Rosie* (tour), *Translations, The Pied Piper, Hobson's Choice* and *The Rivals* (co-production with the West Yorkshire Playhouse).

Other lighting designs include *A Streetcar Named Desire, Dona Rosita* (British premiere), *Oliver Twist, Master Harold and the Boys, Too Much Too Young* (world premiere) and *The Red Balloon* (Bristol Old Vic); *Abolition* (Paines Plough and Old Vic, London); *Inventing a New Colour*, the 1992 Young Writers' Festival and *Outside of Heaven* (Royal Court); *The Glass Menagerie, Entertaining Mr Sloane, Our Day Out* (Sherman Theatre Company); *Woodhouse on Broadway* (BBC TV and Plymouth Theatre Royal); *The Yeoman of the Guard* (D'Oyly Carte Opera Company); the German premiere of *Prometheus* by Scriabin, conducted by Claudio Abbado (Berlin Philharmonic); *Rotterdam Avontur* (Holland); *On the Town* (London Symphony Orchestra at Barbican Hall); *When We Are Married* and *Someone Who'll Watch Over Me* (West Yorkshire Playhouse); *Misery* (Criterion); *Requiem* and the re-light of *Don Giovanni* (Vienna Kammeroper); and *Les Liaisons Dangereuses* (Derby Playhouse).

He has recently lit *The Marriage of Figaro* (Vienna Kammeroper); and Benjamin Britten's *A Midsummer Night's Dream* (Covent Garden Festival). He was also responsible for the lighting design for this year's *Ice Show* at Alton Towers.

VICKI MORTIMER
Vicki Mortimer studied at the Slade School of Art. She has completed four seasons at the Chichester Festival Theatre which included Brecht's *Mr Puntila and his Matti*, Marivaux's *Triumph of Love, Cloud Nine* and *Therese Raquin*.

Productions for the Royal Shakespeare Company include *A Woman Killed with Kindness, The Dybbuk and Ghosts*. For Shochiku Theatre, Japan she has designed *The Eagle Has Two Heads* and *The Lady from the Sea*, and a trilogy of plays for Theatre Project Tokyo (TPT) in Japan in 1993.

Other productions include *As You Like It* (State Theatre of Turkey in conjunction with the British Council); *Arden of Faversham* (Old Red Lion, Islington); *Trios* (Haymarket Theatre, Leicester); *A View from the Bridge* and *The Government Inspector* (Crucible Theatre, Sheffield); *The House of Bernarda Alba* (Gate Theatre); *At Fifty She Discovered the Sea* (Liverpool Playhouse); and *Gorky's The Last* (The National Theatre, Ireland).

Most recently she has designed the Scottish Opera production of *The Turn of the Screw* (Tramway, Glasgow); *Home* (West End and national tour); *Rutherford & Son* (Cottesloe, Royal National Theatre) and a second season of plays for TPT in Japan. Future work includes *The Marriage of Figaro* (Scottish Opera) and *The Threepenny Opera* (Donmar Warehouse).

RUARI MURCHISON
Ruari Murchison studied Biochemistry at Newcastle University before winning an Arts Council Trainee Designer's Bursary in 1981.

Theatre designs include productions of *Old Times, Playing by the Rules, Big Maggie, Translations, Hobson's Choice, Syme, Blithe Spirit*, the world premiere of *The Snowman*, and *The Tempest* (Birmingham Rep); *Oliver!* (York Theatre Royal); *Catch 22* (Sheffield Crucible); *Dark at the Top of the Stairs, Touched, A Chorus of Disapproval* and *My Cousin Rachel* (Derby Playhouse); *The Normal Heart, Prisoners, King Lear* and *Les Miserables – The Play* (Nottingham Playhouse); *Tons of Money* and *London Assurance* (West Yorkshire Playhouse); *Measure for Measure, Educating Rita* and *Sex Please – We're Italian* (Young Vic); *The Fancy Man* (Hampstead Theatre Club); *The Piggy Bank* (Greenwich); *Outside of Heaven, Weldon Rising* (Royal Court); *Cat Walk, Woyzeck* and the award-winning *Sweet Sorrow* (Hull Truck in Edinburgh, London and Los Angeles).

He has designed national tours of *The Entertainer* (Good Company, Northcott) and *Habeas Corpus* (Mobil Touring). Opera work includes *The Fisherman* (Royal College of Music/London International Opera Festival); *The Crucible* (Royal Academy of Music); *Zaza and The Pilgrims of Mecca* (Wexford Opera Festival); *L'Italianna in Algieri* (Buxton Opera Festival); *The Magic Flute* and *A Midsummer Night's Dream* (Covent Garden Festival); and *The Barber of Seville* (Garsington).

NEIL MURRAY
Neil Murray studied Fine Art in Newcastle-Upon-Tyne and Hull and gained a teaching diploma in Birmingham. He works as a director and designer in theatre and dance.

As resident Artist in Theatre at the Birmingham Arts Laboratory, 1973-78, he inaugurated two companies: Performance Group, a cross-art form touring theatre company with a predominant emphasis on contemporary dance, film and the visual aspects of theatre, and The Contemporary Dance Workshop which produced twice-yearly performances using prominent choreographers and dancers as course leaders.

As a freelance designer he has designed for EMMA Dance Co, EMMA Theatre Co, Second City Theatre Co and London School of Contemporary Dance. He was commissioned by the Arts Council to choreograph and design two pieces for Tamara Long and one for Scottish Ballet Moveable Workshop. He staged two large scale community projects *Witches Blood 1 & 2* in collaboration with Alan Lyddiard and a further project at the Tramway, Glasgow for the City of Culture year.

He joined Dundee Rep as Head of Design in 1980 and then became an Associate Director from 1984 until 1992. He also worked freelance for Borderline Theatre Co, Royal Lyceum in Edinburgh, TAG (Glasgow Citizens) and at Queen Margaret College, Edinburgh. He is currently an Associate Director for the Northern Stage in Newcastle upon Tyne.

JOHN NAPIER

John Napier studied at Hornsey College of Art and subsequently at the Central School of Arts and Crafts under Ralph Koltai. He is an Associate Designer with the Royal Shakespeare Company.

Notable productions for the RSC include *Macbeth*, *The Comedy of Errors*, *King Lear*, *Once in a Lifetime*, *The Greeks*, *Nicholas Nickleby*, *Hedda Gabler*, *Peter Pan* and *Mother Courage*. His productions for the Royal National Theatre include Peter Shaffer's *Equus*, later seen world-wide and *Trelawny of the 'Wells'* in 1993. His designs for opera include *Lohengrin* and *Macbeth* (Royal Opera House), *Idomeneo* (Glyndebourne), and *The Devils* (English National Opera).

In the musical theatre, he has designed *Cats*, *Starlight Express*, *Les Misérables* and *Miss Saigon* for Broadway and venues around the world. Other designs in the West End include *Time* and *Children of Eden*.

He designed the *Captain EO* video, starring Michael Jackson, for Disney. He designed and co-directed the spectacular *Siegfried & Roy Show* at The Mirage in Las Vegas, followed by Stephen Spielberg's film *Hook*. Most recently, he has designed *Sunset Boulevard*.

He has won two Society of West End Theatre awards, a BAFTA and four Tony Awards.

FRANCIS O'CONNOR

Francis O'Connor trained at Wimbledon School of Art. He has worked in both the UK and Ireland concentrating particularly on new writing. Designs for new Irish drama include *Wild Harvest* (Druid Theatre, Galway and Dublin); *Silverlands* (Peacock Theatre, Dublin); *The Bread Man* (Gate Theatre, Dublin); *October Song* (Charabanc); and most recently *After Easter* by Ann Devlin (RSC). He has also designed *The Siege of Derry*, a large-scale community play to mark the tercentenary of the siege of the city. Other designs in Britain include productions for the Gate Theatre, Notting Hill, Sheffield Crucible and Helen Edmundson's *The Clearing at The Bush*. Musicals include *Into the Woods* (Singapore) and *The Ugly Duckling* at The Watermill in Newbury.

He has worked extensively in introducing design to both children and adults through his workshops with the Royal Opera and the Royal Ballet Education Departments. He has collaborated with hundreds of children and young adults on creating designs for original operas including *Treasure and a Tale* (Snape Maltings); *New Maureen* (Leicester Haymarket) and *The Boat of*

a Million Years (Bloomsbury Theatre, London).

NICK ORMEROD

Nick Ormerod trained at Wimbledon School of Art. He is Joint Artistic Director of Cheek by Jowl which he founded with Declan Donnellan in 1981. He has designed every production that the company has produced including, most recently, *As You Like It*.

At the Royal National Theatre he has designed *Fuente Ovejuna*, *Peer Gynt*, *Angels in America* and *Sweeney Todd* and at the Finnish National Theatre, *Macbeth* and *Philoctetes*. Plans include *The Rise and Fall of the City of Mahagonny* (ENO) and *Martin Guerre* in the West End. With Declan Donnellan he wrote and directed *The Big Fish*, a short film for Channel 4.

KEITH ORTON

Keith Orton graduated from the Central School of Speech and Drama in July 1992. Theatre work includes *Into the Woods* (Central School of Speech and Drama); *George Orwell* (Lyric Studio, Hammersmith); *Shadowlands* and *The Card* (Sutton Arts Theatre, Birmingham); *Little Shop of Horrors* (national tour); *A Few White Boys Talking* by Ronnie Greer (London New Play Festival, nominated for Best Design); *Steel Magnolias* (Crescent Theatre, Birmingham); *Noises Off* (Highbury Theatre, Birmingham); *The Monster He Made Me* by Michael Butt (Finborough Theatre Club) and *Not, Not, Not, Not, Not Enough Oxygen* (National Student Drama Festival).

He has a long association with the Oldham Coliseum where he has designed *Habeas Corpus*, *Seasons Greetings*, *Educating Rita* and *Sinbad the Sailor* all directed by Warren Hooper; *Our Day Out* directed by Peter Fieldson; *Little Shop of Horrors* directed by Lindsay Dolan; the world premiere of *My Mad Grandad*, by Mike Stott; a community play, *Heart and Soul* and the world premiere of *Bare* by Renny Kropinski. In June 1994 he became Resident Designer at the Oldham Coliseum.

KATE OWEN

Kate Owen trained at the Central School of Art and Design and began working at the Citizens Theatre, Glasgow. She became seduced by alternative and experimental theatre, designing the first productions of many new theatre pieces in the 1970s and 80s.

Theatre designs have included *The Gut Girls*, *Gaslight* and *Jack and the Beanstalk* (Albany Empire); *Circus Moon* (Half Moon); *The Man Who Lit Up The World* (Hackney Empire/LIFT Festival); *On the Verge*, *East Lynne*, *Loot* and *Entertaining Mr Sloane* (Birmingham Rep); *Poppies*, *This Island's Mine* and *Kitchen Matters* (Gay Sweatshop); *Two* (Not the National Theatre); *Stairway to Heaven* (Shared Experience); and *Betrayal* (Two's Company).

Dance and visual theatre designs include *Labelled with Love* (Albany Empire); *Three Pieces* (Extemporary Dance Theatre); *Dirt, Cold Wars* and *Strokes of Genius* (Blood Group); *Crazy Daisy* and *Ordinary Lives* (Laurie Booth). She has directed *The Visitor* and *Familiar Feelings* (Theatre Centre); and *More* (Gay Sweatshop).

DAVID B PALSER

David B Palser trained at the Slade School of Fine Art and has worked extensively in the theatre as a director and a designer.

Recent design work includes *Joan of Kent* (Great Escape Theatre Co); *Romeo and Juliet* (Theatre Royal, Hanley); *An Evening with Gary Lineker* (Maverick Theatre Co); and *First Night*

Nerves (ADC Theatre, Cambridge). Other designs include *Henry II*, *Parallax*, *The Trial*, *Dry Rot*, *Happy Families*, *Solitaire*, *The John Merrick Experience*, *Doctor Faustus*, *Absolute Hell*, *The Boyfriend*, *Dusa, Fish, Stas and Vi*, *Brigadoon*, *Hamlet*, *To My Country A Child* and Stephen Berkoff's *The Fall of the House of Usher* which tours in November 1994 in association with Maverick Theatre Co.

In addition to his work in the theatre, David B Palser is Visiting Lecturer at the Birmingham Institute of Art and Design, Department of Theatre Design.

MICHAEL PAVELKA

Michael Pavelka trained at Wimbledon School of Art. He has worked extensively at the Warehouse Theatre, Croydon where new productions have included *Cheapside*, *Bleached*, *The Fishing Trip*, *The Astronomer's Garden* (also at the Royal Court Upstairs), *Sugar Hill Blues* (also at Hampstead Theatre) and *Playing Sinatra* (also at Greenwich).

Other designs have included *Stepping Out*, *Dames at Sea*, *Cabaret* and *Fashion* (Leicester Haymarket); *The Complaisant Lover*, *Abiding Passions* and *Period of Adjustment* (Watford Palace Theatre); *The Wizard of Oz* (Sheffield Crucible); *The Birthday Party* (Manchester Library Theatre); *The Case of the Dead Flamingo Dancer* (Thorndike and Churchill Theatres); *Entertaining Mr Sloane* (Cambridge Theatre Company) and *Bête Noir* (Young Vic).

His West End credits include *How the Other Half Loves* (Duke of York's); *Holiday* (Old Vic); *Blues in the Night* (Piccadilly and New York), *Robin, Prince of Sherwood* (Piccadilly); *Other People's Money* (Lyric); and *Leonardo – The Musical* (Strand).

In 1993 he designed the Royal Shakespeare Company's production of *The Odyssey* which opened at The Other Place and then transferred to The Pit. Other recent design projects include *Middle-Age Spread* (Palace Theatre, Watford); the touring production of *Same Time, Next Year* (Nuffield Theatre, Southampton); *A Midsummer Night's Dream* and *Twelfth Night* (Library Theatre, Manchester) and *Noel/Cole Let's Do It* (Chichester Festival Theatre).

PERSPECTIVE THREE

Amanda Benwell, Jon Driscoll and Tessa Scott met while studying theatre design at Croydon College. Tessa Scott's pre-college work included constructing exhibitions at the Horniman Museum and scenic construction for the Young Vic Theatre Company. Amanda Benwell had been a researcher and costume maker for the National Youth Theatre summer season and Jon Driscoll had been assistant lighting designer on *Orpheus and Eurydice* for Scottish Opera and *The Barber of Seville* for Opera Northern Ireland.

They all worked in various capacities on West 28th Street Company's production of *The Nativity*, adapted by Tony Harrison from the Medieval Mysteries, but it was on the final production at Croydon College that they came together as designers. They worked with Christopher Cowell (director) and Jonathan Butcher (musical director) on a Surrey Opera production of *Turandot* at the Ashcroft Theatre, Croydon and the Stag Theatre, Sevenoaks.

They are currently working on separate projects: Amanda Benwell on interpreting and making costumes designed by Madeleine Herbert for the British Youth Opera's production of *Eugene Onegin* to be staged at Sadlers Wells; Tessa Scott on constructing and painting the set design by Gerry Livesy

for a tour by Gut Reaction Theatre Company; and Jon Driscoll as production manager for Opera Europa for Puccini's *Gianni Schicchi* and Mascagni's *Cavalleria Rusticana* at Holland Park Theatre.

NIGEL PRABHAVALKAR

Nigel Prabhavalkar trained at the Central School of Art and Design, graduating in 1983 with a degree in theatre design. He was a finalist in the Linbury Prize for Stage Design and his designs for Framework's *The Birds* represented the UK in the 1987 Prague Quadrennial Exhibition of Theatre Design.

Since 1983 he has worked in theatre, opera and dance as well as designing the sets for the conference and music industries. He has designed for Richard Jones, Tim Albery, Jatinder Verma, Kumar Saswat, Ramin Gray and John Turner amongst others. Recent work has included *Landscape Portrait* (Glasshouses); *Message for the Broken Hearted* (Liverpool Playhouse); *All Because the Lady Loves...* (Victoria Worsley); *Wicked Yaar* (Royal National Theatre) the Rover 600 launch and the Technics Music Festival at the Birmingham International Convention Centre.

At the end of the first year of the Theatre Design course it was suggested that he become a lighting designer. With this diversity of interests he has developed an enquiring and filmic approach to his work and not a purely decorative one. Many of his projects are collaborative and allow him to explore fields that are beyond the usual boundaries of the label Theatre Designer.

SAUL RADOMSKY

Saul Radomsky qualified as a fine art teacher in South Africa before coming to England to study theatre design at Nottingham. He has been resident designer at the Northcott Theatre, Exeter, the Cambridge Theatre Company, Hampstead and the Oxford Playhouse Company.

He first worked with director Jonathan Lynn at the Cambridge Theatre Company with whom he has since collaborated on *The Matchmaker*, *Happy End* and *Loot*, with Leonard Rossiter, the musical *Songbook* (which transferred to Broadway), and *Tonight at 8.30* for which he won a SWET nomination. Other productions have included *Strippers* (Phoenix Theatre); *The Italian Straw Hat* (Shaftesbury); *Canaries Sometimes Sing* (Albery); *You Never Can Tell* (Haymarket Theatre); O'Neill's *A Touch of the Poet* (Young Vic and Comedy Theatre); the musical *Budgie* (Cambridge Theatre); *Rick's Bar, Casablanca* (Whitehall Theatre); *Another Time* (Wyndham's); and *Reflected Glory* (Vaudeville).

For the National Theatre he has designed *A Little Hotel on The Side*, *Jacobowsky and The Colonel* and *Three Men on A Horse*, all directed by Jonathan Lynn; for the Royal Shakespeare Company, *Anna Christie*, and for the Chichester Festival Theatre, *Ring Round The Moon*, *The Heiress* and *Getting Married*.

His work overseas has included *Macbeth* and *Whose Life Is It Anyway?* in India; *Awake and Sing* and *Trumpets and Raspberries* in Israel and *Candida* and *The Taming of The Shrew* in Hong Kong.

ADRIAN REES

Adrian Rees trained at Wimbledon School of Art. He has been Head of Design at the Belgrade Theatre, Coventry, since 1987 where he has designed more than 50 productions including *The Hunchback of Notre Dame*, *The Country Wife*, *Blood Brothers*, the much acclaimed 1987 *Coventry Mystery Plays*, *Shadowlands*, *Martin Chuzzlewitt*, *The Curse of the Baskervilles*, *Safe in Our Hands*, *The Importance of Being Earnest* and *Fiddler on the Roof*.

Premieres have included *Guardian Angels* by Julian Garner and *Peggy Buck* by Bill Gallagher. He has designed touring productions of the premiere of Catherine Cookson's *The Fifteen Streets* and *In the Midnight Hour*. Other productions have included the musical *Three Guys Naked from the Waist Down* (Donmar Warehouse); *The Fifteen Streets* (The Playhouse); costumes for *Return to the Forbidden Planet* (Cambridge Theatre); additional costumes for *Buddy* (Victoria Palace); and costumes for *Leonardo* (Strand) and *Pal Joey* for Bob Carlton.

NICHOLAS THOMPSON, RHWL PARTNERSHIP, ARCHITECTS

RHWL was founded in 1961. It is a leading architectural practice specialising in all aspects of theatre design and has worked on over 150 auditoria around the world. The experience gained working with performers, directors and managements led to the formation of the RHWL Arts Consultancy. Led by partner Nicholas Thompson with interior design consultant Clare Ferraby and architects Eric Lawrence and Julian Middleton, the team is involved in every aspect of the design of the building from site selection, brief writing, theatre planning, through to the detailed interior design, graphics and even the design of staff uniforms in order to achieve a total concept.

New regional theatres in the UK include The Crucible, Sheffield; Derngate, Northampton; New Victoria, Woking; Warwick Arts Centre; Towngate, Basildon and The Embassy, Skegness. Refurbished theatres include the Theatre Royal Newcastle; The Alhambra, Bradford; The Lyceum, Sheffield; Theatre Royal, Nottingham; New Theatre, Cardiff; The Haymarket, Basingstoke and the studio theatre reconstruction at The Crucible, Sheffield. The team's work in London includes the Prince Edward Theatre, the Old Vic, the Duke of York's, and the Donmar Warehouse, the Royal Centre at Nottingham, the Anvil at Basingstoke, and currently the new Manchester Concert Hall.

Current contracts include a study for a disabled people's art centre in Manchester; the Chicken Shed Children's Theatre in North London; the reconstruction of the Metropol Theatre in Berlin and auditoria in Duisburg and Stuttgart with Cameron Mackintosh.

POLLY RICHARDS

Polly Richards trained in theatre design at Nottingham Polytechnic, graduating in 1990. Since then she has designed sets and costumes for a variety of small- and middle-scale theatre companies, touring (predominantly) to schools, village halls and studio theatre venues.

Her design work has included *The Mandrake*, *Rapunzel*, *The Adventures of Pinocchio* and *A Passion for the Countryside*, a promenade community show (all for Oxford Touring Theatre Company); *Journey* and *Message in a Bottle* (Theatr Iolo, Cardiff), *Animal Farm*, *The Good Person of Sichuan*, *King Oedipus* and *The Hunting of the Snark* (Leicester Haymarket Studio Theatre) and two Forum Theatre shows, *Sex Acts* and *Deaf Voices* for the London Bubble Theatre Company.

More recent work includes *About Face*, a devised and masked piece (Salisbury Playhouse Theatre); and co-designing the 1993 summer season for the London Bubble Theatre. In 1994 she spent three months learning to carve and weave masks with the Dogon Tribe in Mali, West Africa. She plans to continue this research and to integrate it with her theatre work in the years to come.

CHRISTOPHER RICHARDSON

Christopher Richardson studied interior design under Sir Hugh Casson at the Royal College of Art where he gained a silver medal for experimental theatre design. He was part of the team winning the *Prix d'Etranger* at the Paris Biennale in 1965 and later at the Liberec Symposium in Czechoslovakia. He taught design and then Drama at Uppingham School, for which he designed and ran the Uppingham Theatre. He also continued with his theatre design, creating sets for shows starring Mollie Sugden, Max Wall, Griff Rhys Jones and Rowan Atkinson and acting as consultant on various theatre schemes including the Arts programme for the Taft School in Connecticut, USA. He runs the Pleasance Theatre Festival as part of the Edinburgh Festival, is a director of the Festival Fringe Society and has designed many plays for the theatre both in the UK and abroad.

In 1986 he became an associate of MEBP and started Theatre Futures with John Marsh and John Faulkner, since when he has worked on all the group's theatre projects. Theatre Futures has recently refurbished the Young Vic Theatre in London and completed several school theatres. Current engagements include the refurbishment of the Opera House in Jersey and the Century Theatre, Keswick. He is a member of the Society of Theatre Consultants and currently chairs the Society of British Theatre Designers.

MARSHA RODDY

Marsha Roddy trained at the Wimbledon School of Art. Not content with simply being regarded as a theatre designer, her work adopts the broader definitions of production designer and art director.

Having reached the West End early in her career (with Carib Theatre's production of *Amen Corner*) she moved into film. As assistant art director for First Floor Features, Holland, she worked on the films *Oh Boy*, *My Blue Heaven* and *Northerners* and a variety of commercials.

Her interest in promoting high quality, intelligent theatre for children has seen her relationship continue with Quicksilver Theatre for Children (*Bedlam*, *The Three Secrets of Serendip*, *No 3 Pied Piper Street*), Theatre Centre (*The Magic Shoes*), The Crucible Theatre (*Gorbelly*, *Waiting for Godot*), and Ragdoll Productions (*Rosie and Jim's Big Theatre Adventure*). She has also worked with Felgate Productions' children's programmes for the BBC and with two films for Leda Serene Productions, for the BBC's Shape Shifters Series.

HELENA RODEN

Helena Roden studied theatre design at Wimbledon School of Art, then began designing small-scale touring productions for which the size of the van was as significant as the performance space. Working with companies such as Graeae, Spare Tyre, Little Women and Theatre of Black Women, she learnt a lot about issue-based work, budget control and reaching the audience. Her frustration with the small scale of some of this work was temporarily satisfied in 1990 when she designed the set for a Wembley Stadium spectacular of Indian film stars, loads of colour and a real elephant.

In 1988 she joined a group of women artists – The All Ladies Number One Brush Team – and began to make work that had a longer life and more personal significance, but still retained an understanding of interaction with the public, for example an installation called *The Dresses*, which explored girlhood, and more recently a commission to create a 30m-long sculpture on Folkestone seafront.

Her current design work on projects such as *West Side Story* by Wandsworth Prison and Pimlico Opera and new music-theatre pieces with Glyndebourne Education and the English National Opera's Baylis Programme, have allowed her to use the vision that she has developed in an 'art' context whilst incorporating the collaborative community-based aspect of her earlier career.

MAGDALEN RUBALCAVA

Magdalen Rubalcava studied in Dublin and at the Central School of Art and Design and works as a designer in film, dance and theatre. Her work in the theatre has included *Havadana*, *1919 An Incident*, *Exiles in the Forest*, *Bhavni Bhavai*, *Roundheads & Peak Heads*, *The Government Inspector* and *Oedipus Rex* (Tara Arts); *Tartuffe* and *The Little Clay Cart* (Royal National Theatre); *Heer Ranjha* (Theatre Royal Stratford East and tour); *The Tempest* and *Troilus & Cressida* (Contact Theatre, Manchester and tour) and costumes for *September Tide* (King's Head, Islington).

Work in the field of dance includes *Edge* (Sue MacLennan); *Breaking Images*, *Raj Quarter* and *Alpha Beta Gamma* (Extemporary Dance Company); and *Déjà Vu* and *Arcadio* (Motionhouse).

She has worked as assistant to Consolata Boyle on the following films: *Widow's Peak*, *The Secret of Roan Inish*, *The Secret Rapture*, *The Woman who Married Clarke Gable*, *Troubles*, *December Bride*, *The Irish RM*, *When Reason Sleeps*, *Sarah Curran*, *Playboys* and *Into the West*.

CATHY RYAN

Cathy Ryan studied Fine Art at Bristol Polytechnic and post-graduate Theatre Design at the Bristol Old Vic Theatre School. Design work has included *Strange Fruit*, *City Echoes*, *Take My Husband* and *It's a Bobby's Job* (Liverpool Playhouse); *The Conduct of Life*, *Struggle of the Black Man and the Dogs*, *Vera Baxter*, *The Struggle* (Gate Theatre, Notting Hill); *Streetwalkers* (Bush Theatre, London); *Weissman and Copperface* (Traverse Theatre, Edinburgh); *Loot* (Swan Theatre, Worcester); *Heimerbeit* (Battersea Arts Centre Young Directors Award); *Fen and Masterpieces* (Theatre Royal, Stratford East); *Pretend We're Friends* (Quicksilver Theatre for Children); *The Cunning Little Vixen* (The Baylis Programme of Opera Workshops ENO); *The Marriage of Figaro* (Pimlico Opera); *Thark*, *When the Wind Blows*, *Dangerous Corner* and *David Copperfield* (New Victoria, Stoke); *Way Past Cool* (Royal Court Young People's Theatre); *Flat 4D*, *The Gap*, *Stop the Rot* and *What a Life* (Cardboard Citizens and Deaf Theatre Forum at the London Bubble). Film and television work includes *Rif Raf*, *Ladybird Ladybird*, *Young Soul Rebels*, *Institute Benjamenta* and *Brookside*.

ALAN SCHOFIELD

Alan Schofield has designed and painted scenery since childhood, starting with toy theatres and later converting henhouses, haylofts and any other space he could find into improvised theatres. He designed for Sunday school pantomimes and then for the Clayton and Droylsdon Amateur Dramatic Society.

On leaving school in the late 1950s the future of professional theatre looked bleak so he decided to follow his second passion, photography, as a career. He became involved in film-making and was then Head of the NPL Film Unit in Teddington for 21 years. During this period he continued to work in amateur theatre, designing for opera, drama, ballet, musicals and pantomime, gradually becoming increasingly involved, semi-professionally, with youth theatre. In 1989 he became resident designer and scenic artist at Elmhurst Ballet School, the UK's oldest vocational performing arts school.

NETTIE SCRIVEN

Nettie Scriven studied Drama and Sociology at Birmingham University and has an MA in Fine Art from South Glamorgan Faculty of Art and Design.

She has worked extensively as a theatre designer in the UK and specialises in designing for new writing and with theatre companies that devise work. She is an associate of Hijinx Theatre Company in Cardiff. Other work has included *Rooms* (Glasshouses Dance Co); *Dreaming It Up* (Theatre Centre); *The Snow Spider* (Sherman Theatre); *The Lost Child*, *Plague of Innocence*, *Noah's Daughters*, *Can't Pay, Won't Pay* (Sheffield Crucible); *Hamlet* (Contact Theatre); *The Waltz* (West Yorkshire Playhouse at the Henry Moore Foundation Gallery). She has also worked for Skottes Music Theatre in Sweden, Made-in-Wales Stage Co, Roundabout TIE, Perspectives Theatre Company and Women's Theatre Group.

She is Lecturer in Theatre Design at Nottingham Trent University, a board member of Theatre Centre, London and a founder member of the theatre and lighting designers co-operative agency, the Designers' Formation.

ASHLEY SHAIRP

Ashley Shairp trained in theatre design at Trent Polytechnic from 1983-86 after which he worked as an occasional designer, prop-maker and painter.

He worked with Paul Kondras at the London Bubble in 1988 and then at the Duke's Playhouse, Lancaster. Designs here included *'Tis Pity She's a Whore*, *Bring Down The Sun* and outdoor promenades in the park of *Much Ado About Nothing* and *The Tales of King Arthur*.

Freelance work has included designs for Solent People's Theatre, The Liverpool Everyman, Theatre Foundry, Derby Playhouse, Chester Gateway, The Forum (Wythenshawe), Cleveland Theatre Company and further shows for the Duke's. He also designed *The Wizard of Oz* and *A Day in the Life of Joe Egg* (The Everyman, Cheltenham); *Alfie* and *Cabaret* (The Octagon, Bolton); and very excitingly collaborated with James Mackie and Ludus Dance Company on *Timetrax* and *The Spark*.

Recent projects have included working within the design department on Mersey Television's *Brookside*, designing dance pieces for the BBC Education Department with Ludus; and working as a dresser at Granada Television.

JULIET SHILLINGFORD

Juliet Shillingford trained at Ravensbourne and Croydon Colleges of Art, receiving a degree in fine art and a diploma in theatre design. She was awarded an Arts Council Bursary in 1983.

She has been associate designer at both the Redgrave Theatre, Farnham and the Library Theatre, Manchester designing over 30 productions in five years. Freelance work has included a national tour of *An Ideal Husband*,

Stepping Out, Salt of the Earth, Cinderella and *French Paste* (Oldham Coliseum); *Joking Apart, It's a Girl and Crazy People* (Library Theatre, Manchester); *The Haunting of Middle Mause* (Perth Theatre); *Saint Oscar* (Leicester Haymarket Studio); *Matchgirls* and *Babes in Arms* (Beck Theatre, Hayes); *Rhinoceros, Fertility Dance, Sauce for the Goose, A Christmas Carol, Out of the Sun, Around the World in Eighty Days, Sly Fox, The Three Musketeers* and *Jungle Book* (Nuffield Theatre, Southampton). She recently designed the ballet *Misa Criolla* (Churchill Theatre, Bromley).

DAVID SHORT

David Short studied design at the Wimbledon School of Art and on the English National Opera design course. He won an Arts Council Bursary which took him to the Northcott Theatre, Exeter and then to the Royal Court in London. In 1973 he won the George Devine Award.

He has worked extensively for the Royal Exchange Theatre, Manchester, designing set and costumes. He designed costumes for *The Corn is Green, Treasure Island, Hope Against Hope, Moby Dick, The Alchemist, A Midsummer Night's Dream, The Voysey Inheritance, She Stoops to Conquer* (also national tour) and *Donny Boy*. He designed the set and costumes for *One Flew Over the Cuckoo's Nest, The Plough and the Stars, Street Captives* (Corn Exchange); *Class K, Entertaining Mr Sloane, Jack and the Giant, The Glass Menagerie, Romeo and Juliet, A View from the Bridge, Blues for Mister Charlie* (1993 Manchester Evening News Best Design Team Award with Ace McCarron and Rebecca Watts), *The Comedy of Errors, Little Murders* and more recently, *Smoke*. In 1983 he was awarded the Gold Medal for work submitted by the Society of British Theatre Designers at the Prague Quadrennial.

TIM SHORTALL

Tim Shortall works as a designer for theatre, dance and television. His theatre work has included *900 Oneonta* (Old Vic Theatre and Lyric Hammersmith); *Body and Soul* (Albery); *A Cook's Tour* (Shaftesbury); *We Like Ike* (Royal Festival Hall); national tours of *The Importance of Being Earnest, Moments of Weakness, Body and Soul, The Decorator, Candide* and *Relatively Speaking*. He was Head of Design at the Thorndike Theatre, Leatherhead for three years.

Dance work has included *Private City* and *Track and Field* (Royal Ballet, Sadlers Wells); *Sonata in Time* (Scottish Ballet); *Uncertain Steps* (Introdans, Holland and Ontario Ballet Theatre); *After I Drank Sorrow* and *Classified* (both for Dance Advance); *Merry Widow* (Netherlands Dans Theater, Springplank); *Rhyme Nor Reason* and *Party Gam* (Norwegian National Ballet).

Work for the Dutch television company NOS TV has included *The Factory, Six Turkish Folkpoems* (which was selected to represent Holland in the Tokyo International Design Exhibition) and *The Nightingale*, with the Dutch National Ballet, which was awarded the RAI Prize for Visualisation at the Prix d'Italia '83.

ANNIE SMART

Annie Smart trained at the English National Opera Design Course (now The Motley Design Course) in 1979-80. As Resident Designer at the Haymarket Studio in Leicester she designed *George Dandin, Medea, Woyzeck* and *The Bald Prima Donna*. In 1985-6 she was Head of Design at the Liverpool Playhouse. Productions elsewhere have included, for Joint Stock, *Fen* (Almeida, Royal Court and Public

Theatre, New York); *Fire in the Lake* (Edinburgh Festival) and *A Mouthful of Birds* (Royal Court); *Woman in Mind, Easter* (Haymarket, Leicester); *The School for Scandal, Hiawatha* (Bristol Old Vic); *True West* (Shared Experience) and *The Swan* (Traverse). She has also designed for the Royal National Theatre.

RAE SMITH

Rae Smith trained at the Central School of Art and at the Glasgow Citizens' Theatre. She has worked as a designer in Scotland, America and in former Yugoslavia for the arts collective Neue Slowenische Kunst, The Mladinsko Theatre, Red Pilot and the National Theatre, Subotica.

In England, designs for Theatre de Complicité include *The Visit* and *The Street of Crocodiles* (co-production with Royal National Theatre). Other credits include *The Magic Flute* (Opera North); *A Midsummer Night's Dream* (Royal Lyceum, Edinburgh); *The Europeans* (The Wrestling School); *Gormenghast* (David Glass); *Shameless* (Opera Circus) and *Death of a Salesman*, directed by Matthew Warchus (West Yorkshire Playhouse).

For the Royal Shakespeare Company she has designed *Henry VI, The Battle for the Throne* for the 1994-95 regional tour starting at The Other Place in Stratford. She has received two awards for design to support working sabbaticals in Indonesia and Japan.

IAN SOMMERVILLE

Ian Sommerville studied at the Royal Scottish Academy of Music and Drama. He has designed lighting for Opera North, English National Opera, Sadlers Wells Opera and Scottish Opera. His lighting for dance includes *Shoes* (London Contemporary Dance Theatre) and *Nutcracker* (Adventures in Motion Pictures). Recently he has begun working in theatre, lighting *Moscow Stations* and *Poor Super Man* (Traverse Theatre, Edinburgh); *HRH* (Theatr Clwyd) and *The Lady from the Sea* (West Yorkshire Playhouse and Lyric Hammersmith).

He is also a set designer and has designed *Poisoned Silence* (Opera North) – the company's first design-led project – and *Tosca* (Crystal Clear Opera). He has been strongly influenced by his collaborations with director/designer Tom Cairns and the painter Howard Hodgkin.

GEOFF SPAIN

Geoff Spain trained at the Bristol Old Vic Theatre School before starting his professional career at the Mercury Theatre, Colchester with that well known thriller *The Bat*. He has been resident lighting designer at the Wolsey Theatre, Ipswich, since 1989. Credits here have included *The Three Sisters, Shadowlands* and *No Man's Land*. He was previously theatre technician (and projectionist) at the Torch Theatre, Milford Haven. Recent work includes *All My Sons* for the Oxford Stage Company on tour.

MICHAEL SPENCER

Michael Spencer has been a professional theatre designer for 11 years during which time his work has encompassed theatre-in-education, community theatre, commercial touring, repertory and opera. He most recently designed the national tour of *Macbeth* for Welsh National Opera. His work with Harrogate Theatre's artistic director, Andrew Manley, stretches back over seven years and 20 productions including this season's *The Merchant of Venice* which opened in October 1994.

He became the first Theatre Design MA graduate in 1991 and now lectures

at Central St Martin's School of Art and Design whilst continuing his freelance career.

JACKIE STAINES

Jackie Staines studied for a Higher National Diploma in Lighting Design, graduating in 1985. She is currently resident lighting designer at the Stephen Joseph Theatre, Scarborough. Here her designs have included *June Moon, Same Time Next Year, The Village Fête, Rutherford & Son, To, Neville's Island, Rocket to the Moon, Feed, Love Off The Shelf, The End of the Food Chain, Gaslight, Penny Blue, Two Weeks with the Queen, Conversations with my Father,* and by Alan Ayckbourn *Invisible Friends, Callisto 5, This is Where We Came In, Confusions, My Very Own Story, The Norman Conquests, Dreams from a Summerhouse, Haunting Julia,* and *The Musical Jigsaw Play*. She has also been responsible for lighting several seasons of Studio shows and has lit tours and transfers of a number of productions for the same company, including *Two Weeks with the Queen* at the Royal National Theatre.

On a freelance basis, Jackie has lit *Blithe Spirit, Macbeth, Turn of the Screw* and *A Midsummer Night's Dream* (Harrogate Theatre). She occasionally writes for Lighting and Sound International magazine and is the North Eastern area representative for the Association of Lighting Designers.

ANDREW STORER

Andrew Storer studied Scenography at Wimbledon School of Art and graduated in 1981. He is best known for his dance designs for the American choreographer Robert North, with whom he has collaborated on over 20 productions. These include three full-length ballets *Elvira Madigan* (Danish Royal Ballet, 1987 & Gothenburg Ballet, 1992), *America* (Nevada Dance Theatre, 1990 & Gothenburg Ballet, 1991) and Prokofiev's *Romeo et Juliette* (Grand Theatre Geneva, 1990).

He has also designed for Ballet Rambert, English National Ballet, London Contemporary Dance Theatre, Hanover Ballet, Ballet du Nord, Teatro dell' Opera Rome, Ballet de Santiago, The Spoleto Festival, Stuttgart Ballet and Teatro Regio Turin and has collaborated with the choreographers, Christopher Bannerman, Michael Clark, Robert Cohan, Mark Morris, Wayne Sleep and Janet Smith.

His designs for television include *For My Daughter* by Robert North (Danish Royal Ballet/Danmarks Radio/ZDF); *Lonely Town, Lonely Street* (Ballet Rambert/RM Arts/Virgin Classic Video) and the lighting for the *European Summit Gala* (SCO/BBC 1992) and the *Sound Bytes II* concerts (BBC 1993). Current projects include *Romeo and Juliet* (Gothenburg), *Gaité Parisien* (Geneva) and a new ballet based on the Faust legend.

TAD:14

Sam Anderson, Alan Bain, Louise Beck, Jason Brooks, David Burrows, Steve Bush, Tamsin Currey, Josh Ford, Rachel Heavens, Kate Hind, Peter Lindley, Georgia Lindsay, Andrea John and Cheryl Roberts are the group of designers making up TAD:14.

TAD:14 was formed in 1991 from the first year student group of the BA (Hons) Technical Arts Design Course at Wimbledon School of Art and their course leader, David Burrows. This was the beginning of an on-going commitment to, and experiment with, non-hierarchical collaborative design processes.

In the Spring of 1991 TAD:14 designed the settings for the German professional premiere of Willy Russell's

Blood Brothers, directed by Phil Young and the British premiere of Alfred de Musset's *On Ne Badine Pas Avec l'Amour* (*Don't Fool With Love*) directed by Jean-Marc Lanteri (The French Institute, London).

Various smaller combinations of the group have since designed *The Poor of New York* by Dion Boucicault, directed by Jonathan Martin (Lilian Baylis Theatre, Sadlers Wells, 1993); *The Train* directed by Hilary Westlake (E15's theatre, 1993; produced by Imagination) and the British premiere of Georg Kreisler's *Tonight: Lola Blau* directed by Phil Young (Old Red Lion, Islington, 1993).

The students have now graduated and are working, or seeking work, in the various areas of their combined expertise including set, costume, lighting and sound design for theatre, film, television and exhibitions.

IAN TEAGUE

Ian Teague trained at Trent Polytechnic (now Nottingham Trent University). He started work in 1982 as assistant designer at Liverpool Everyman Theatre and has since designed for various repertory theatres including Cheltenham Everyman, Dukes Lancaster, Torch Milford Haven and Liverpool Everyman.

Designs for community touring projects have included work with Forest Forge, Durham Theatre Company, Theatre Venture and Pocket Theatre, Cumbria. Most of his work in recent years has been in Theatre in Education including projects with Greenwich and Lewisham Young Peoples Theatre (GYPT), Tie Break, Clwyd Outreach, Breakout TIE, Action Transport, Y Touring and Wolsey TIE, Ipswich.

He chairs the British Actors Equity Designers Committee.

FRAN THOMPSON

Fran Thompson studied visual art and drama at the University College of Wales. Much of her career has been spent designing for Shakespeare and new writing, working with, amongst others, the directors David Thacker, Anthony Clarke and Gwenda Hughes. She began as Associate Designer at the Wolsey Theatre, Ipswich then became Head of Design at the Palace Theatre, Watford where she designed *Lulu* and *Chance Visitor* by Alexei Arbuzov. She designed the opening production of *The Importance of Being Earnest* at the Wilde Theatre, Bracknell and a series of new plays at the Nuffield Theatre, Southampton: *Dead Men* by Mike Stott, *Working Class Hero* by Bob Mason and *Just a Kick in the Grass* by Richard Ireson.

Elsewhere she has designed *Comedians* (Liverpool Everyman); *All's Well That Ends Well* (Leeds Playhouse); *Picture Palace* (Women's Theatre Group); *Twelfth Night* (Theatre Royal, Stratford East); *Safe in Our Hands* (West Yorkshire Playhouse); *Memoirs of a Survivor* (Salisbury Playhouse Studio); *All My Sons, My Mother Said I Never Should* (Birmingham Rep); *Julius Caesar, Romeo and Juliet, Enemy of the People, Measure for Measure, The Price* and *All My Sons* (Young Vic) and for the Royal Shakespeare Company *Pericles* (Swan Theatre and The Pit), *Julius Caesar* (The Other Place and international tour) and *Coriolanus* (Swan Theatre).

MARK THOMPSON

Mark Thompson's work in the theatre has included *The Scarlet Pimpernel* (Chichester and Her Majesty's); *Cabaret* (Strand); *The Sneeze* (Aldwych); *Ivanov* and *Much Ado About Nothing* (Strand); *A Little Night Music* (Piccadilly); *Shadowlands* (Queen's Theatre and Broadway); *Joseph and the Amazing*

Technicolor Dreamcoat (Palladium and Canadian, Australian and American tours); Six Degrees of Separation (Royal Court and Comedy Theatre); Hysteria and The Kitchen (The Royal Court).

He has designed Measure for Measure, The Wizard of Oz, Much Ado About Nothing and The Comedy of Errors (Royal Shakespeare Company); Volpone, Betrayal, Party Time and Butterfly Kiss (Almeida Theatre); The Wind in the Willows, The Madness of George III, Arcadia and Pericles (Royal National Theatre). Arcadia also transferred to the Haymarket Theatre.

Opera designs include Montag aus Licht (La Scala, Milan); Falstaff (Scottish Opera); Peter Grimes (Opera North); Ariadne auf Naxos (Salzburg); Il Viaggio a Reims (Royal Opera House, Covent Garden); Hansel and Gretel (Sydney Opera House) and Two Widows (English National Opera).

Mark has won the Olivier Award for Best Design on three seaprate occasions: Wind in the Willows (1990), also winning the Plays and Players and the Critic Circle Design Awards; Joseph and the Amazing Technicolor Dreamcoat and The Comedy of Errors (1992) and Hysteria (1994). He also won a Green Room award in Australia for the set design for Hansel and Gretel (Sydney Opera House).

Recent work includes Don Quixote (Royal Ballet, Covent Garden) and costumes for the film version of The Madness of George III. Future work includes Pique Dame (Metropolitan Opera, New York); and What the Butler Saw (Royal National Theatre).

TRIADIC (to be updated)
Triadic is a partnership between a designer, a director and a printmaker. Their work is design led and often starts from sculptural and environmental concerns.

Jeremy Longmore studied Fine Art and Theatre Design at Birmingham Polytechnic and the Slade School. Howard Shaw trained as a psychologist and at the School of Communication at the Polytechnic of Central London. Penny Wells studied Fine Art at Exeter University. She is currently an artist-in-residence in Shropshire.

In Autumn 1995 Triadic will design and direct Purcell The Fairy Queen bringing together music, masques, dance and choral work.

KENDRA ULLYART
Kendra Ullyart was born in County Durham. She graduated from Nottingham Polytechnic in 1987 with a BA Hons in Theatre Design. Her career began at the Contact Theatre in Manchester as an Assistant and later as Resident Designer. Shows there included Galileo, Metamorphosis, The Red Balloon and Fool for Love for which she received a Manchester Evening News Design Award.

Since turning freelance in 1991 she has designed Blood Wedding (Royal National Theatre); A Midsummer Night's Dream (Sheffield Crucible and National Theatre of Athens); Just So, Pecong and Pinchy Kobi and the Seven Duppies (The Posse at the Tricycle Theatre); Dickens' Women (Hampstead Theatre and Duke of York's, London); White Woman Street (Bush Theatre, London and Peacock Theatre, Dublin); An Inspector Calls (Bolton Octagon); Hair (Old Vic); The Beggar's Opera (Royal Shakespeare Company); Romeo and Juliet (Tampere Theatre, Finland) and Otello (Essen Opera House, Germany).

Recent credits include The Hostage and The Venetian Twins (Royal Shakespeare Company at the Barbican) and the West End transfer of Once on This Island (Royalty Theatre).

JOE VANEK
Joe Vanek joined the National Theatre in Dublin as Director of Design in January 1994 following a ten-year association with theatre and opera in Ireland. Major productions designed for its two theatres have included: in the Abbey, St Stephen's Green and Brian Friel's Dancing at Lughnasa (also seen at the Royal National Theatre in London, in New York and world-wide) and Wonderful Tennessee, Moses Rock and Chamber Music and for the Peacock, John Banville's adaptation of The Broken Jug.

For the Gate Theatre in Dublin, productions include A Woman of No Importance, The Recruiting Officer, Heartbreak House, Innocence, Peer Gynt, The School for Scandal, The Threepenny Opera and Brian Friel's Molly Sweeney (also at the Almeida, London). Also in London he has designed numerous West End and fringe productions and during his career in England has held three Head of Design posts in regional theatres. Recently he designed Sienna Red for the Peter Hall Company and The Matchmaker at Chichester.

His opera designs have been seen at Opera North, WNO, ENO, Wexford, in Israel and in Copenhagen for the Royal Opera. Major productions have included Cosi Fan Tutte, Don Giovanni, La Cena delle Beffe, Turandot, The Duenna, Don Pasquale, Ariane and Bluebeard, Rigoletto, Caritas and The Love for Three Oranges.

In 1993 he received two Tony nominations for Dancing at Lughnasa on Broadway.

HUGH VANSTONE
Hugh Vanstone trained at the Northcott Theatre, Exeter where he started lighting shows in 1982. Recent credits have included The Card (UK tour); La Bohème (English National Opera); Butterfly Kiss (Almeida); Once On This Island, Copacabana, Leonardo and Moby Dick (West End); Macbeth (National Youth Theatre); Moll Flanders (Lyric Hammersmith); Scrooge (UK tour and Australia); The Ugly Duckling (Watermill, Newbury).

Hugh has collaborated with Andrew Bridge as the Associate Lighting Designer for the London and international productions of Aspects of Love, Five Guys Named Moe, The Hunting of the Snark and Joseph and the Amazing Technicolor Dreamcoat.

He also works with the design company Imagination creating lighting designs for industrial launch spectaculars, special events and architectural projects.

GRAHAM WALNE
Graham Walne has lit over 500 productions, is an author, writer and presenter of two lighting videos, a lecturer at major drama schools, a partner in two theatre consultancies – having personally led over 50 projects – and the co-founder and chairman of the AETTI the body delivering Scottish and National Vocational Qualifications for backstage staff.

His lighting design credits range from six plays in a pub attic to the Bolshoi Ballet at the Royal Albert Hall, the subject of his display in this exhibition. He has worked with the Bolshoi both in the USA and in Moscow. Other clients have included the Paris Opera and Boston Opera, the Royal Cultural Centre Jordan, the Opera Company of Israel and the Opera Company of the Philippines. In the UK he has lit over 100 touring and 50 West End productions including works at Sadlers Wells, the Theatre Royal Drury Lane and the Westminster Theatre. He has numerous pantomime and cabaret designs to his

credit including work at the Green Room, Café Royal and the Dorchester Hotel. He has also designed the lighting for several events such as the Lutyens Festival and the Royal Academy of Arts Summer Ball.

ANTHONY WARD
Anthony Ward's designs for repertory theatres have included A Comedy of Errors, A Streetcar Named Desire, Donna Rosita, Oliver Twist and Lady Windermere's Fan (Bristol Old Vic); Medea, Death and the King's Horseman, The Winter's Tale, The Parasol and costumes for Born Yesterday (Royal Exchange, Manchester). He has also designed productions in Derby, Leicester, Nottingham, Plymouth, Worcester and York.

For the Royal Shakespeare Company he has designed A Midsummer Night's Dream, King Lear, The Tempest, Artists and Admirers, The Winter's Tale, The Alchemist, The Virtuoso and Troilus and Cressida.

In London he has designed Oliver! (London Palladium); Assassins (Donmar Warehouse); A Hard Heart (Almeida Theatre); the set for The Rehearsal (Almeida and Garrick Theatre); and Sweet Bird of Youth and Napoli Millionaria (Royal National Theatre).

In opera he has designed Tosca (De Vlaamse Opera, Antwerp); Manon Lescaut (De Vlaamse Opera, Antwerp and Opera de Paris Bastille); La Bohème, Yolande & The Nutcracker, L'Etoile and Gloriana (Opera North) and The Nutcracker for Adventures in Motion Pictures (Sadler's Wells). Gloriana was also performed at The Royal Opera House.

CHRIS WATTS
Chris Watts has been involved with professional theatrical events for 15 years. He has worked with most of the major companies in England including a period as technical and electrical supervisor for the Plymouth Theatre Royal. Between 1987 and 1990 he taught theatre lighting at Northwestern University in Evanston and Chicago and then Cornell University in Ithaca, New York. He returned to England and took up a position with Theatre Projects Consultants in 1990, where he has worked on such projects as Glyndebourne Opera House, the Savoy Theatre, London and the Walt Disney Concert Hall in Los Angeles. He is also a guest lecturer at Croydon College. He is currently Secretary of the Association of Lighting Designers and a member of the Association of British Theatre Technicians and the United States Institute of Theatre Technology.

WELFARE STATE INTERNATIONAL
– Engineers of the Imagination
Welfare State International was founded by John Fox and Sue Gill in 1968 and has for 25 years been at the forefront of arts practice and development both in Britain and abroad. The company has gained an international reputation for the creation of extraordinary site-specific, celebratory events, but is equally at home working on a small-scale, one- or two-person, community-based event.

Years of research has led the company to the concept of applied vernacular art. They have created prototypes that challenged existing cultural patterns, whilst offering creative alternatives. Their work is context-led; the poetry is determined by occasion, geography and social needs.

IAN WESTBROOK
Ian Westbrook trained in Theatre Design at Nottingham Trent University. His first show, one of many for the Lord Delfont Group, was with Lenny Henry and Cannon and Ball. After

seasons in Nottingham, Leicester and Plymouth he began a long-term association with the Norwich Theatre Royal.

He is the founder of the scenic design company 3D Creations based in Great Yarmouth and his designs and sets have been seen in New York, Amsterdam, Vancouver, Berlin, Paris and London's West End.

Each year he designs the Cromer Seaside Special end-of-pier shows – the last traditional summer show in existence. In 1994 he designed eight shows, including Brighton Rock, and created a huge set in Neo-Classical style for the Earl of Leicester's estate at Holkham Hall, Norfolk for a pageant and son et lumière.

LOUISE ANN WILSON
Louise Ann Wilson studied Theatre Design at Nottingham Trent University, graduating in 1993. Her entry to the Linbury Prize for Stage Design in November 1993 was one of 15 selected for an exhibition at the Royal National Theatre.

She has a keen interest in site-specific work and has worked as both designer and performer on several projects in Nottingham, including The Game at King David's Dungeon, Nottingham Castle (Bruised Back Theatre company); Gormenghast by Mervyn Peake, in Nottingham Castle grounds; Don't Go Near the Water in The Basement Studio (The Eastwicks Theatre company) and Rites Rules Wrongs devised and also directed by Louise in The Park Tunnel.

Theatre design work includes Drink the Mercury a devised show by the Belgrade, Coventry TIE (Nottingham College of Performing Arts), Hood in the Wood, co-designed with the director, Bill Mitchell (Roundabout TIE Company); Measure For Measure (Clarendon College, Nottingham); The Edible City and Natural Forces (Humberside TIE tour); Falling Angels (Meeting Ground Theatre Company at the Leicester Haymarket Studio, and national and international tour); and in 1995, Threads from the Past (West Yorkshire Playhouse TIE tour).

ANDREW WOOD
Andrew Wood studied theatre design at Nottingham Polytechnic (now Nottingham Trent University) and graduated in 1991. He worked as a freelance designer before joining Contact Theatre in Manchester as assistant designer in August 1992. His freelance designs have included West Side Story and Tennessee Rose (National Student Theatre Company at the Edinburgh Festival); When The Dance Is Over (Raw Cotton Young People's Theatre Company) and The Conquest of the South Pole (Theatre Factory). Productions for Contact's Youth Theatre included The Wedding on the Eiffel Tower and I Too Speak of the Rose. He has designed the Young Playwrights Festival at Contact Theatre for the past three years and is a founder member of Bruised Beak performance group.

HAIBO YU
Haibo Yu trained as a theatre designer in China, where he executed a number of designs for theatre and television productions. He obtained a scholarship to study at the University of Leeds in 1986 and then transferred to a postgraduate course at Central St Martin's School of Art and Design. He has been involved as a design assistant on a number of theatre and television productions, among them The Way South at the Bush Theatre, John Brown's Body at Tramway, Glasgow and Suffer the Little Children for BBC2. He is currently a tutor at St Mary's University College and has designed more than 20 productions both in the College Theatre and the Studio.

INDEX OF DESIGNERS

THEATRE DESIGN UMBRELLA

PARTICIPATING ORGANISATIONS

THE ASSOCIATION OF BRITISH THEATRE TECHNICIANS

Formed in 1961, the ABTT advances and represents the technical interests of the theatre through information, advice, education and debate. It is a registered charity and a membership organisation, open to professionals and others interested in the technical and craft aspects of theatre.

The Association draws up codes of safe practice. Through these and other publications and through in-service training courses, it disseminates information, advice and recommendations.

Through its committees, the ABTT monitors and aims to influence new standards and regulations affecting the industry and it provides an advisory service for those involved in the planning of new theatres and the conversion or refurbishment of existing buildings.

It organises an annual trade show in London and a biennial show in the North, in addition to a programme of members' meetings and seminars.

47 Bermondsey Street, London SE1 3XT
Tel: 0171 403 3778

THE ASSOCIATION OF LIGHTING DESIGNERS

The Association of Lighting Designers is the professional body representing lighting designers in all fields within the United Kingdom and abroad. A voluntarily run association, it exists to provide a resource and forum for discussion and development of artistic and creative aims amongst designers from the fields of Theatre, Television, Architecture, Education, Industrial and Corporate Presentations and Manufacturing.

There are five main membership categories in the ALD: Full, County, Associate, Student & Corporate.

The membership includes leading lighting designers from Britain and indeed other parts of the world. Corporate members enjoy access to an accurately targeted database of lighting professionals.

The ALD holds regular members meetings and activity days. Recent and planned meetings include: Show Briefings, Product Demonstrations, Master Classes and Discussion Groups.

The ALD publishes a monthly news magazine called 'Focus' giving details of meetings, associated events and lighting news. In addition, an education update is published once a year and gives training and education news, including details of new courses and programmes for lighting design across the world.

The ALD is a constitutionally formed Association run by an Executive Committee who report to the general members.

3 Apollo Studios, Charlton Kings Road,
London NW5 2SW
Tel: 0171 482 4224

BRITISH ACTORS EQUITY ASSOCIATION

Equity is delighted to be associated with the Designers' Exhibition in the Manchester City of Drama Year. It welcomes the opportunities afforded by this showcase of members' talent and creativity, and applauds the continuing high levels of professionalism shown by designers even in the current, often difficult, financial climate.

Equity currently has over 500 designers on its designers' register. It has negotiated agreements with all the major employers' groups: the Theatrical Management Association, the Society of London Theatre and the Independent Theatre Council.

These agreements cover everything from billing to model expenses, from copyright to minimum fees.

There is a full time Organiser and an Assistant available to help with queries connected with the Equity Designers' contracts. The Organiser will also represent Designer members in the event of contractual disputes with managers.

In addition, all the normal services available to members can be used by designers. Of these, the advice on tax and DSS claims provided by the Welfare Benefits Officer is particularly useful. There is also a legal service provided to members who have legal problems connected with their work. This is much used by members, especially those with personal injury problems.

Equity welcomes and encourages the involvement of its designer members, and will continue to strive to maintain and improve its service to them.

Guild House, Upper St Martin's Lane,
London WC2H 9EG
Tel: 0171 379 6000

THE SOCIETY OF BRITISH THEATRE DESIGNERS

The Society of British Theatre Designers was founded in 1971 by John bury, with Ralph Koltai, Nicholas Georgiadis and Timothy O'Brien. It started life with the object of deciding on the most appropriate union to negotiate for designers. Since then it has developed and diversified and now has a wide membership. It aims to enhance the standing of British theatre design at home and abroad in many different ways. One of these is to organise every four years an exhibition of theatre design which in part represents Britain in Prague at the international Quadrennial. It also arranges seminars and forums for discussion and development of professional practice. Designers are easily isolated by their work. Their Society puts them in touch with one another, with painters and sculptors, and with those working in theatre in other countries.

47 Bermondsey Street, London SE1 3XT
Tel: 0171 403 3778

Upper Campfield Market
CASTLEFIELD · MANCHESTER

UPPER CAMPFIELD MARKET · CASTLEFIELD · MANCHESTER